From the CROSS *to the* MOUNTAIN

A 90 Day Devotional to Take You from
Calvary to the Ascension of Christ

Darlene Rose Busse

Printed in Canada
ISBN: 978-1-4866-1752-4

Word Alive Press
119 De Baets Street Winnipeg, MB R2J 3R9
www.wordalivepress.ca

WORD ALIVE
—P R E S S—

MIX
Paper from
responsible sources
FSC   FSC® C103567

Cataloguing in Publication information may be obtained from Library and Archives Canada.

Contents

SPECIAL MENTIONS

In this fast-paced age of electronics, I still have a computer that came over on the Mayflower. So when my long-time friend Susanna Munro offered to type my manuscript, I was so thankful. I am blessed to have her as a friend. I can honestly say that I don't know how she did it, as my writing is atrocious and sometimes unreadable—even to me. I would not like to guess how many hours she spent typing and re-typing, and I am so thankful for her. I ask the Lord to richly bless her.

I'm also thankful for Shauna Friesen, the Director of Care and Administration at my church. She's done so much for me.

I'm thankful for family and friends who have prayed for me, especially my sister Ann Holderbein and friend Carol Dunham, who pray for me every day.

A special thanks to my nephew, Duane Ashton, who shared a personal story with us. He's a special blessing to me, and from time to time he calls me from Virginia to see how I'm doing and to pray for me.

Finally, without the Lord in control of my life there would be no book, and I would still be a broken vessel instead of a new creation. Take Jesus down from the cross and walk with Him. He will restore you.

FOREWORD

I can't remember the first time I met Darlene. It seems as though she's always been a part of my life. With my mom living quite a distance away, Darlene and I formed a very special, precious bond—one based on love and great respect. I look up to and admire Darlene's heart and passion for God and His people. She's a beautiful example of what living a God-centered life looks like.

The first time she put her arm around me and said, "I pray for you every morning," I thought, *People always say stuff like that, but ...* Then Darlene said it again the next week, and the next. It finally sank in that I had a prayer warrior in my corner. Knowing that this incredibly strong, faithful woman was actually praying for me changed my life. I felt a new sense of strength. It was something different than I'd ever felt before. I was no longer scared to fail. Even though I knew there would be times that I would stumble and things would happen that were out of my control, I would have God and Darlene there to catch me when I fell. God would be there for me spiritually, and Darlene would be there as His hands and feet to dust me off, encourage me, and tell me to keep trying and give me a loving push when I dug my heels in and didn't want to.

I believe that Darlene received a calling from God to write *From the Cross to the Mountain*, her second book. I had the privilege of reading Darlene's first book and was moved by her powerful story. Her words invoked such a range of emotion in me that I felt like I was actually living the story. *From the Cross to the Mountain* will be just that—a spiritual pilgrimage that will take our hearts and souls to places only God can lead us. Day by day, we experience in both subtle and profound ways what God's love and grace mean in our lives. I would follow Darlene anywhere, and I can't wait to find out where we end up at the end of "a journey."

Shauna Friesen
Director of Care & Administration
East Side Church of God
Swift Current, Saskatchewan, Canada

INTRODUCTION

A number of years ago, I finished the manuscript for my book, *Two Alone*. The last few paragraphs described a scene from a Billy Graham movie:

> Picture it! A huge, thriving, twentieth-century city, complete with skyscrapers, businesses, malls, and homes. There are thousands of cars on the freeways hurrying to get home. People are standing in line to board buses or trains! People are everywhere! Hustle and bustle! Horns are honking! People are laughing and talking, kids are playing!
>
> To the left of the city, high on a hill, Jesus was hanging on a cross. He was battered and bruised, and He was bleeding. His feet and hands were adorned with nails and blood. His back was bare and bleeding from being whipped. Drops of blood dripped from under the ... crown of thorns.
>
> As I looked at Him, all the chaos and clamour of the city was drowned out by the deafening silence of Jesus suffering for

me. He took my pain, my sin, so that I can live. He loves me that much!

The movie ended there, but the story didn't end when he died. That day He won the war for me when He took the keys to death and hell, and rose victoriously to defeat sin. Thank you, Jesus: You saved my Life![1]

The manuscript for *Two Alone* was finally finished. I had written everything I felt the Lord wanted me to say. I put my pencil down and left Jesus hanging there!

This book is a journey that starts at the foot of the cross. It has no chapters; there are only steps that turn into many miles on the road to maturity in the Lord. So let's put on a pair of comfortable walking shoes and go on this journey together. We will meet with the living Lord!

---

[1] Darlene Rose Busse, *Two Alone* (Baltimore, MD: America House Book Publishers, 2000), 259–260.

Day One

THE TORRENT BELOW THE CALM

"… the torrent would have swept over us, the raging
waters would have swept us away."
(Psalm 124:4b–5)

My husband and his friend Allan love to fish. Sheila and I like to be on the boat, but fishing … not so much. But when salmon fishing on the Pacific Ocean was in the plans, we happily agreed to go along.

Telegraph Cove is a quaint little fishing village on the northern end of Vancouver Island, British Columbia. It has been renovated but keeps its antique charm, and thousands of tourists enjoy it each year. We hired a fishing guide, and all five of us headed out to deep waters. It had rained earlier, so the ocean was a bit choppy. The fishing boat seemed small to me, and feeling the depth of the water below made me a little uneasy. My life jacket was my "security blanket."

We had gone out quite a few miles when the guide stopped the boat beside an amazing ocean phenomenon. We observed a huge, round area of completely calm water. The guide explained that it was a rip current, commonly called a "riptide." I read that it's caused by the opposing pull of the tides. A swift circular undercurrent beneath the surface water causes the tides to revolve around each other. The calm surface can fool you, and if you get caught in it, you can drown. Small shrimp are a diet staple for salmon, so these riptides are swarming with them. They go in, get disoriented because of the turbulence, and become trapped. The salmon then gather and have a "feeding frenzy."

Riptides parallel life. We appear to be calm on the surface. We put on our happy faces and make it look like all is well with the world, but underneath run torrents of daily living that swirl around and want to destroy our peace of mind. Calm can be found! Jesus tells us of peace: "… *in Me you may have [perfect] peace. In the world you have tribulation and distress and suffering, but be courageous [be confident, be undaunted, be filled with joy; I have overcome the world…*" (John 16:33, AMP)

Day Two

THINGS END

"There is a way that appears to be right,
but in the end it leads to death."
(Proverbs 14:12)

Our summer Sunday morning routine: coffee on the patio, change clothes, then off to church. The conversation was normal until I heard, "I don't love you anymore. I want a divorce!" Thirty-two years together and it was all over in one sentence. I couldn't believe what I'd just heard, and I cried, "What?" He wanted out? It didn't make sense to me, because a few months earlier he told me that he loved me.

We had invited friends out for lunch after church, so we kept that commitment. Robots can function and maintain the appearance of normality; however, that day started a three-and-a- half-month facade. I cried almost all of the time, and I cried myself to sleep most nights. We lived completely different and separate lives in the same house. What seemed right to my husband led to the "death" of our marriage. At sixty-two years of age, I started a long journey from brokenness to complete reliance on and trust in the Lord. Things end! New things begin!

PHANTOM SEMI-TRUCK
"For he will order his angels to protect you wherever you go" (Psalm 91:11, NLT).

FROM THE CROSS TO THE MOUNTAIN

I had tickets for a three-day southern gospel music celebration in Red Deer, Alberta. Driving alone had never been a problem, but this time I was emotionally numb and a little fearful. I tried to put a CD in so I could listen to some music, but I couldn't even remember how to turn it on. "Please help me, Lord!" I pleaded. I finally remembered what to do and wept as I listened to God's Word in song.

In my rear-view mirror I noticed a semi-truck following me. For many miles he would come up behind me and then fall back—never passing me. I thought that maybe the Lord had sent that semi to follow me and show me that He was with me wherever I went. I decided to find out. He continued to follow me—left lane, right lane, slow down, speed up, or pass a vehicle. He was my shadow! An angel had been sent for me. He followed me for two hours and then was gone. God gave me peace for the rest of the trip, and I thanked Him for His protective and comforting angel.

HOMELESS

*"But Jesus replied, 'Foxes have dens to live in, and birds
have nests, but the Son of Man has no place
even to lay his head.'"*
(Matthew 8:20, NLT)

When I got home from Alberta, we listed our house for sale. It sold almost immediately, so we only had a short time to relocate our lives. We experienced a flurry of activity involving a garage sale, dividing possessions, and packing. My husband moved into his office, but I had no place to live. There were absolutely no apartments available within my price range.

One could say that Jesus was homeless. All through the Gospels we read about His lifestyle. He walked everywhere. He walked all through Galilee and Judea, to Samaria and through Jericho. He walked along the seashore, to deserted places, and up hills and mountains. The one time He didn't walk occurred when He rode a colt into Jerusalem on Palm Sunday (Luke 19:28–40). Jerusalem was the walk that ended at the cross.

Jesus never stayed in one place too long. In the Gospels, many verses start with, "He went into the house," or "He left the house." He stayed in people's homes. He stayed with Simon the leper, Simon Peter at Capernaum, in houses in Bethany and Samaria, and many other homes:

"And in the daytime He was teaching in the temple, but at night He went out and stayed on the mountain called Olivet [Mount of Olives]" (Luke 21:37, NKJV).

Many commentators believe that the sermon on the mount and the beatitudes (Matthew 5:1–12) probably covered several days of preaching. I imagine that Jesus and the crowd of five thousand plus stayed on the mountain at night.

Jesus ate at Mary and Martha's house. He also ate at Peter's home and Matthew's house with Zacchaeus and other tax collectors. He ate with the rich and the poor, with scribes and Pharisees. Before He ascended to heaven, He cooked breakfast for His disciples on the seashore. He said, *"Come and have breakfast"* (John 21:12). Can you imagine the Son of God cooking breakfast for you? Jesus left His home in heaven to become homeless here on earth, but He knew His earthly home was only temporary. His heavenly home is eternal.

I prayed for a miracle, and at the last minute an apartment that had been spoken for became available. I was so thankful that the Lord in His goodness provided for me "a place to lay my head."

Day Four

TEARS IN A BOTTLE

"You have seen me tossing and turning through the night.
You have collected all my tears and preserved them in
your bottle! You have recorded every one in your book."
(Psalm 56:8, TLB)

I pleaded with God to lead my husband back to me, so when I was told that he was with another woman—and that he had been with her while we were together—I felt my heart leave my body and come back shattered. I felt that God had turned His back on me, and now I was alone.

One day in 2009 I received an e-mail from an undisclosed sender that perfectly described my life: "I remember that I have to get up, breathe, put one foot in front of the other, eat, drink, and fight off the heartache, tears, and depression and try to get through this one day." The image of God, the collector of tears, actually collecting my tears in His bottle eventually showed me that He intimately cares for and loves me. Just imagine Him looking at each tear, writing down what it represents, and saving it until He provides His loving answer ... which He does in His own time and in His own way. My part was to trust Him.

King David wept before the Lord many times and for many different reasons. Each Psalm that he wrote either starts or ends with him praising and thanking God for His goodness and mercy. When he wrote that

God was "collecting his tears in a bottle," he believed it and trusted God in all things and for all things.

We can go two ways when we're broken-hearted. We can draw into a deeper relationship with the Lord, or we can go through a desert and dry up until we understand that He will heal our hearts if we draw close to Him.

King David wrote: "... *This one thing I know: God is for me!*" (Psalm 56:9b, TLB).

Day Five

A Song in the Desert

The passage found in Ezekiel 37:1–10 is titled "A Valley of Dry Bones" in my Bible. God gives Ezekiel a vision for the Israelites who were exiled to Babylon. The dry bones represent God's people, who believe all hope is gone for them to ever go home again. In this scripture, God promises to bring Israel back to life.

I parallel this scripture to my life. I too was dried up, spiritually and emotionally dead in the "valley of dry bones." I asked the Lord, "Will I ever be whole again?" Then the Lord reached into my soul and "spoke to" my dried-up spirit and told me that He was going to "breathe life" into my soul so that I could live again. I heard the word of the Lord, and my bones began to "rattle and shake" and attach themselves to my empty soul. But I still wasn't whole. Then with the "wind" the Lord breathed life into me and I lived again. I "stood up" and was alive and whole!

While I was lying in the "valley of dry bones," praying for life, the Lord gave me a song.

"A Song in the Desert"

1. I wandered in the desert; my soul was parched and dry. My spirit was so thirsty. No water was nearby. When I searched for Jesus, He gave a song to me.

2. My eyes they could not see Him; I did not hear His voice. My words of praise were empty; my heart did not rejoice. As I longed for Jesus, He gave a song to me.

3. I was alone, forsaken, God's Son my only friend. I had to leave the desert or dry up in the wind. When I asked my Savior, He quenched my thirst again.

Chorus: Is there a song in the desert, Lord? Dark clouds covered my sky each day. When I searched for the Master's face, Calvary came down and rescued me!

In the desert we feel emotionally and spiritually dead. Life has "kicked us in the stomach," so to speak, and we are empty. My life had been emptied of trust and faith, but I knew I wanted to see the desert bloom again. In Arizona in the spring I have seen the desert bloom, and it's a beautiful sight. The Lord is living water. He gave me a drink, and I was alive again. Like the song says, "Calvary (Jesus) came down and rescued me." If you're in a desert, ask the Lord for a drink of His living water. He will quench your thirst!

Day Six

ENOUGH

Jesus said, "*So do not worry about tomorrow; for tomorrow will care for itself. Each day has enough trouble of its own*" (Matthew 6:34, NASB).

When I survived the desert and felt like I had my life back, reality hit. Life happens to everybody, and it's not always pleasant. For many months I was extremely exhausted. I had no appetite, so I lost weight. After numerous CT scans, ultra-sounds, and biopsies, I received my results. When I heard the words, "You have thyroid cancer," I wanted to run home, write out my will, and plan my funeral. Two surgeries, numerous radioactive iodine injections and drinks, and five years later, I was cancer free. King David stated, "*But God is my helper. The Lord keeps me alive!*" (Psalm 54:4, NLT). The Lord in His goodness let me live.

The verse, "Each day has enough trouble of its own," is a true statement. My lists of troubles are small compared to the unbelievable heartaches some people endue. At that time, though, it seemed that every area of my life was being attacked. My divorce was final. My car needed to be replaced. I had apartment, job, family, and friend problems. My television, computer, and numerous small appliances had died. Within a short period of time, my brother, sister, and sister-in-law passed away.

I said, "Enough already, Lord!" and wondered what would happen next … and if it would ever end.

When I stopped feeling sorry for myself and focused on the Lord and what He went through for me, my "stuff" was just that—stuff. I learned to be thankful in all things. That's not an easy thing to do, but with a new way of looking at problems, and an attitude adjustment, the Holy Spirit stepped in and assured me that it would all work out. I truly was blessed. The Lord gave me my life.

When troubles came and all was gone, the Lord was there. Many times it felt like all I had left was Jesus, and when I totally surrendered to Him, it became clear that the Lord was enough. Life happens, troubles happen, but the Lord is always there.

Day Seven

FEAR AND DREAD

*"Do not be afraid of the terrors of the night,
nor the arrow that flies in the day."*
(Psalm 91:5, NLT)

When I was a little girl, I was afraid of being alone and of strange noises in the dark of night. Mom and Dad slept with their bedroom door open, so when fear overtook me, I tiptoed to their open door and sat on the floor, next to the wall. I whispered, "Mom … Mom," but she didn't answer. After several tries, I gave up. I could hear them breathing and that calmed me down enough to eventually go back to bed and to sleep. Now when I'm fearful I whisper, "Oh Lord!" *"I sought the Lord, and He heard me, And delivered me from all my fears"* (Psalm 34:4, NKJV). And so He does!

We all have fears at times, because fear is a natural instinct. Adult fears vary. Some fears concern family, job security, health issues, or natural disasters such as earthquakes, forest fires, floods, or tornados: *"So we will not fear when earthquakes come and the mountains crumble into the sea"* (Psalm 46:2, NLT). The writer of this Psalm tells us to trust the Lord, because no matter what happens, He is with us.

When ten scouts were sent to explore the Promised Land before the Israelites went in, eight of them came back in fear. They spoke of giants and walled cities. Unfortunately, they forgot that God had promised victory in all they did if they didn't rebel against Him. Moses spoke to the people of Israel and said, "... *Dread not, neither be afraid of them* [the inhabitants]" (Deuteronomy 1:29b, KJV).

The disciples were in a boat when a strong wind came up, and they were being tossed around on high waves. Jesus came to them walking on the water, and they were terrified: "*But Jesus spoke to them at once. 'Don't be afraid,' he said. "Take courage. I am here!*" (Matthew 14:27, NLT).

When fear turns to dread, it can be paralyzing. I've learned that I can trust the Lord to calm me because He is in front of me, behind me, and beside me. When I'm too afraid to take a step, He carries me!

Day Eight

REVERENT FEAR AND WISDOM

*"It is a fearful thing to fall into the hands
of the Living God."*
(Hebrews 10:31, TLB)

Fortunately, God loves us: *"There is no fear in love. But perfect love drives out fear, because fear has to do with punishment. The one who fears is not made perfect in love. We love because He first loved us"* (1 John 4:18–19). The Bible challenges us to have a healthy respect that will end in awe of God as we seek His will for us.

God isn't up in heaven with a big stick waiting for us to make a mistake, hoping to beat us up. If we let Him have His way with us and obey Him, we have no reason to fear Him. He didn't make His commandments to destroy us, but to guide us in living a life that honors and glorifies Him. Should we not have a reverent fear of a God who can part the Red Sea, shred buildings into "toothpicks" during a tornado, and with an earthquake move Japan eight feet to the east and shift the earth's axis four inches? Reverent fear means that I should worship God the Creator, honor His holy name, obey His commandments, respect His authority, love Him, and be in awe of His mighty power.

"The fear of the Lord is the beginning of wisdom, and the knowledge of the Holy one is understanding" (Proverbs 9:10, NKJV). We live in the information age, the age of knowledge. Anything we want to know,

we can find on the Internet, Facebook, Twitter, or other social media outlets. Within a few seconds, we have all the information we need. But if we use that knowledge and forget God, we're on a scary path.

We don't always make wise decisions. A perfect example of this can be seen when we're warned not to drive in a flooded area after a storm. We don't know if the road is washed away underneath or if the car will stall and trap us, yet we often hear about people needing to be rescued by first responders, who have to put their own lives at risk. Unfortunately, some cars are washed away and people drown. Not wise!

In our society today, many do not respect authority of any kind, and many have no fear. There seems to be little wisdom and little understanding. Let us be wise, worship and love God, and respect His authority.

Day Nine

MASKS OR TRUTH?

*"He who believes in Me, as the Scripture has said, out of
his heart will flow rivers of living water."*
(John 7:38, NKJV)

When something blocks the flow of a fast-flowing river with a strong current, the river will make a new path around the obstacles. I have read that a river can be invisible, go underground so to speak, and show up again downstream—sometimes with a stronger flow and current.

We humans are like a river. When we come up against "obstacles," we tend to put on a mask and drop out of sight until we can face the new course of our life. I call it a protection mask, because we can't face the truth that we are devastated. Many of us suffer privately because we want to hide our pain.

Jesus said, "… *If you abide in My word, you are My disciples indeed. And you shall know the truth, and the truth shall make you free*" (John 8:31b–32, NKJV). I had to tell myself the truth. My marriage was over, and I had to let it go. My veil of self-protection was removed, and I was finally set free.

If we let the Lord into our pain and circumstances, He will shine through. "*But we Christians have no veil over our faces; we can be mirrors that brightly reflect the glory of the Lord*" (2 Corinthians 3:18a, TLB). As soon as I let the glory of the Lord shine through, my mask came off.

I had forgotten that the Lord saw my pain and that I couldn't hide anything from Him. He wanted only the best for me. Paul affirms that truth: "*And we know that God causes everything to work together for the good of those who love God and are called according to His purpose for them*" (Romans 8:28, NLT). When God says He'll work it out … He will … because He cannot, and will not, lie. I believe He only wants what's best for me. "*God is not human, that He should lie … does he speak and then not act? Does he promise and not fulfill?*" (Numbers 23:19).

Like a river, my life took a new course. Now when someone asks me how I'm doing, I can honestly say, "I am good!" I don't need to pretend behind a mask. I truly hope that Jesus is reflected on my face and that I am a mirror of the Lord.

Day Ten

GOD'S TIMING

*"There is an appointed time for everything. And there is
a time for every event under heaven."*
(Ecclesiastes 3:1, NASB)

This verse tells me that all things related to time are under God's control.

The rent for my apartment kept increasing, to the point where I couldn't afford it anymore. Each week I combed the newspaper for places with lower rent, but to no avail. One day I had a doctor's appointment regarding follow up cancer treatments in Saskatoon, many miles north of where I lived. I wasn't familiar with the streets there, so I decided to take the bus. I met a lady on the bus who told me about a new, low rental, seniors' complex. She lived there, but she said that they weren't advertising yet. When I got back home, I went to their office, viewed some apartments, and totally loved a duplex I saw; however, another lady had first chance on it. I prayed and friends prayed, and the Lord blessed me with the gift of a brand new duplex. The one I wanted! *"So let us come boldly to the throne of our gracious God. There we will receive his mercy, and we will find grace to help us when we need it most"* (Hebrews 4:16, NLT).

This large seniors' complex where I live is made up of three separate areas. One area of condos serves lunch every day, and they were looking for a person to go in for about three hours a day to be a server for the seniors eating there. One day while paying my rent, the office staff asked me if I would be interested in the job. Serving lunch to seniors for three years has been the highlight of my life. Precious people!

A similar scenario occurred when I had a broken blind and made a trip to the office to report it. I left my car running because I was just going to slip into the office for a minute. To my horror, I heard a knock coming from under the hood. The car was only two years old, so there shouldn't have been any knocking. I took it to the dealership where I'd bought it, and the service manager said I needed to leave it there to be fixed. I had planned to go to Alberta that weekend and was told that the car would probably have left me stranded on the highway. Fortunately, it was under warranty. Many people would say that it was all a coincidence, but I say it's the Lord's perfect timing. I trust God's timing. He is never too early or too late, and He has never let us down!

Day Eleven

BAGGAGE

"… let us strip off anything that slows us down
and holds us back …"
(Hebrews 12:1, TLB)

One Sunday morning my pastor gave an illustration about carrying the weight of baggage. Two guys were mountain climbing. One guy carried a backpack that was full of "stuff." As he climbed, the load became very heavy, and he said he couldn't go on. Wisely, his climbing partner reached over and with his knife cut off the straps. The backpack fell off, giving him the strength to climb to the top. "… *but I focus on this one thing: Forgetting the past and looking forward to what lies ahead*" (Philippians 3:13b, NLT).

When my children and grandchildren accompanied me to Hawaii to my nephew's Naval Change of Command ceremony, we took a lot of suitcases along. On our way back, we had to change planes in Vancouver, British Columbia, and connect with another flight to Calgary, Alberta. In the Vancouver terminal, my daughter tried to get somebody—anybody—to take our luggage so it could be transferred to our connecting flight. Nobody would even speak with her, so in complete frustration she stuffed our luggage on an already-bulging baggage carrier. It all took too long and we had to run to our gate. In Calgary, three flights and many hours later, our luggage finally arrived.

So it is with our personal baggage—if it's not lost, it will come back to us.

Webster's Dictionary defines baggage as "luggage" or "suitcases." Our personal luggage can be filled with anger about job loss, abuse, infidelity, betrayal, bitterness towards someone, emotional injuries, insecurities, and numerous other items. Wherever we go, we take our minds, thoughts, and memories with us. Unless we unpack and give all the contents to the Lord and let Him cut off the load, we will never have peace. Unfortunately, all too often we pack our bags, fill our backpacks, and take another trip. Let's unpack, cut the cords, and look ahead to getting to the top of the mountain so we can see the beautiful view.

Day Twelve

What Chains?

Paul says, "*It is for freedom that Christ has set us free. Stand firm, then, and do not let yourselves be burdened again by a yolk of slavery*" (Galatians 5:1). Paul was in a Roman prison in actual chains on what we call "death row," but his thought was, *What chains?* He didn't see the chains; he only saw opportunities to speak about his love for the Lord Jesus. The chains didn't keep him from praying for believers. He wrote letters of encouragement to Christians everywhere. He didn't pray for the Lord to remove the chains, but to be bold and without fear, and to say the right words to all he spoke to. He took his mind off the chains and focused on the Lord. Paul looked at Jesus, not his chains.

When I took classes on public speaking, I was told that sometimes we can get an idea or theme from magazine pictures. I found a picture in an advertisement of a man from the fashion world who worked for "The House of Givenchy" and moved to "The House of Gucci." It was a heart-stopping, eye-popping, two-page picture in living color. The man was tightly wrapped from top to bottom with heavy, black, link chain. All that was visible were his head, the top part of his shoulders, and his feet. That picture provided a perfect example of how we can be kept in chains, and it's always in my mind.

Today many are in chains of bondage. It could be mental health issues, drug and alcohol abuse, physical abuse, bad attitudes, unhealthy relationships, poverty, health issues, hate, pride, sexual immorality, or any other number of personal problems that keep us locked up in chains. With the Lord's help we can break the chains of whatever bondage is wrapped around our souls and holds us captive. When we pray and ask the Lord to break our chains, He will set us free and will be able to work in and through us.

"I run in the path of your commands, for you have broadened my understanding" (Psalm 119:32). *"O Lord, you have freed me from my bonds [chains], and I will serve you forever. I will worship you and offer you a sacrifice of thanksgiving"* (Psalm 116:16–17, TLB). Erase the picture of full body chains and live free in a new picture … chain free!

A thought: When a caterpillar breaks the chains of its cocoon, it emerges as a beautiful butterfly, healthy and free.

Day Thirteen

TWENTY-FIRST CENTURY WOMEN

The woman in Proverbs 31:10–31 was an excellent woman in all ways, but women today, in my opinion, pass her by far. The commentary in my Bible provides an overview of the woman in Proverbs:

> She had, "strong character, great vision, many skills, and great compassion ... She was an excellent wife and mother, manufacturer, importer, manager, realtor, farmer, seamstress, upholsterer, and merchant. She had strength and dignity and reverenced God."[2]

Have things changed for women today? Yes and no. I believe many women are strong in character and steadfast. Most are wise, but of course there are still women who chose unwisely. We too are skilled, knowledgeable, and compassionate. We have some excellent wives and mothers, but today it's more difficult for single parents who have to be both mom and dad. Unfortunately, some live in poverty. We have

---

[2] *Life Application Study Bible, NLT* (Wheaton, IL: Tyndale House Publishers, Inc., 1996), 1022.

divorcees and widows who still contribute to society, community, and church. Many women today are the bread winners and skilled enough to occupy any job the workforce has to offer. They work as accountants all the way through the alphabet to welders.

One huge difference today is that we live in the Information Age. We have information at our fingertips in seconds with the aid of the Internet, e-mails, texting, Facebook, twitter, and other resources. In spite of all this information, we still behave like some Old Testament women.

Some today, as in the past, are nasty ladies, but we hope that they will meet Jesus and let Him enter their lives and change them.

Another significant difference concerns women's role in the church. In centuries past, women weren't allowed to participate in any "temple" activities or be involved in any way. Today there is no area of the Lord's work that women aren't involved in. My friend Shauna leads a women's ministry team at our church called Women of Worth, W.O.W. Their goal is to give purpose, vision, and value to women; to grow; to develop and transform relationships with the Lord, family, church, community and to uplift and encourage. God has gifted women leaders who are committed to help develop these God-given gifts and to give glory and honor to Him. We are twenty-first century women of worth.

Day Fourteen

THE FRAGRANCE OF PRAISE, WORSHIP, AND THANKFULNESS

"For we are to God the fragrance of Christ …"
(2 Corinthians 2:15, NKJV)

When God places the scent of Jesus in our lives, we carry His aroma with us. I will always remember the first time I got off the airplane in Hawaii. The beautiful fragrance of flowers was with us everywhere we went. That's the way we are to share the aroma of our Lord.

King David wrote: *"Praise the Lord; Praise God our savior! For each day he carries us in his arms"* (Psalm 68:19, NLT). During a very hurtful time in my life, my grandkids gave me a huge teddy bear to hold in my arms. It felt good. There is healing power in God's arms, for which we praise and thank Him.

"Therefore, let us offer through Jesus a continual sacrifice of praise to God, proclaiming our allegiance to his name" (Hebrews 13:15, NLT). Jesus sacrificed His life for us. Let's give praise back to Him for loving us enough to suffer and die for our salvation.

"No matter what happens, always be thankful, for this is God's will for you who belong to Christ Jesus" (1 Thessalonians 5:18, TLB). When things are good, we need to be thankful. When things are bad, we also

need to be thankful, because God is behind the scenes working things out for us. Lord, help us to be thankful for everything; it could be worse.

"*Then King Jehoshaphat bowed low with his face to the ground ... worshiping the Lord*" (2 Chronicles 20:18, NLT). In today's language, we could say he was on his face before the Lord. We don't need to be in a church with a full orchestra or a worship team to worship the Lord— He's everywhere and can be worshiped wherever we are, because He is spirit. Worship is in the condition of our hearts towards Him.

> Once a king of England entered a room where some British noblemen were gathered. As they stood to show their respect, he said, "Sit down. You are my friends. I am not the Lord." One nobleman replied, "If you were the Lord, we would not rise to our feet, we would fall on our knees."[3]

If you find it hard to see God's awesomeness and greatness, just gaze at the sunsets. I see colors I've never seen before, and I believe are not yet named.

All that I am, all that I have, all that I am yet to become, is a gift from God. How can I not praise Him? When we're intimate with the Lord, we praise, worship, and thank Him in one accord for His glory. Be a fragrance to Him.

---

[3] Millie Stamm, *Be Still and Know* (Grand Rapids, MI: Daybreak Books, Zondervan Publishing House, 1978), December 18.

Day Fifteen

UNDER HIS WINGS

*"He shall cover you with His feathers, and under His
wings you shall take refuge; His truth shall be
your shield and buckler* [armor]*."*
(Psalm 91:4, NKJV)

"*How precious is your loving kindness, O God! Therefore the children of men put their trust under the shadow of Your wings*" (Psalm 36:7, NKJV). King David wrote that God carries us in His arms every day, and now he talks about being in the shadow of, or under, God's wings. How safe we are and how much God loves and protects us!

David said, *"… I will hide beneath the shadow of your [God's] wings until the danger passes by*" (Psalm 57:1b, NLT). The storms of life can produce some fiery trials, but if we let God shelter and protect us, He will keep us safe while the storms pass over us.

I saw a news clip on television a while ago about a forest fire in the US that had raged through a mountain growth. After the fire was out, some firefighters went in to look for hot spots. They spotted something strange, so they went to investigate. They found a hen that was burned black and was, of course, featherless. They knew the hen was dead, but as they watched they saw the hen move a little. One firefighter picked it up. Under her were some baby chicks, safe and untouched by the fire.

They were safe because their mother gave her life to protect them. Jesus did the same for us. He gave His life so we can live.

Jesus spoke of Jerusalem and how much He cared for His people, the Jews. He wept because they would not come to Him: "… *how often I have longed to gather your children together, as a hen gathers her chicks under her wings, and you were not willing*" (Matthew 23:37). Fortunately, we Gentiles have been grafted into the root of David:

> *But some of these branches from Abraham's tree—some of the people of Israel—have been broken off. And you Gentiles, who were branches from a wild olive tree, were grafted in. So now you also receive the blessing God has promised Abraham and his children, sharing in the rich nourishment from the root of God's special olive tree.* (Romans 11:17, NLT)

Today both Jews and Gentiles have the opportunity to hide under God's protective wings. He sees no difference if we are His children. We can fully trust Him for our protection if we seek shelter in Him.

Day Sixteen

TRUST

God brought the Israelites to the edge of the Promised Land. All they had to do was go take it. Twelve spies were sent to explore the land and only two trusted in God.

> ...Caleb tried to quiet the people as they stood before Moses. "Let's go at once to take the land," he said. "We can certainly conquer it!" But the other men who had explored the land with him disagreed. "We can't go up against them! They are stronger than we are." (Numbers 13:30–31, NLT)

So God sent them back out to wander in the wilderness for forty years.

> ... why did they (Israelites) stop trusting God ... They were afraid. Often we do the same thing. We trust God to handle the smaller issues but doubt His ability to take care of the big problems... Don't stop trusting God ... He brought you this

far and won't let you down now. We can continue trusting God by remembering all He has done for us."[4]

"*Because you trusted me, I will give you your life as a reward. I will rescue you and keep you safe. I, the Lord have spoken!*" (Jeremiah 39:18, NLT). That is a promise from God that can't be broken. He spoke it, and it is so. He knows what will happen today and tomorrow, and if our todays and our tomorrows are looked after, only trust should remain.

Do we trust Him when everything that could go wrong, does? How do we react when our health fails, or we are betrayed by a friend? Do we doubt God's promise when a child rejects us, or a spouse leaves us or passes away? How about when we lose our job or our home, or when we pray and it seems like God isn't listening? Maybe we become like Peter, who trusted Jesus enough to walk to Him on the water until he looked around and saw the waves and took his eyes off the Lord and began to sink. Jesus said to Peter, "*O you of little faith, why do you doubt?*" (Matthew 14:31, NKJV). So too it is with us. When we take our eyes off Jesus and stop trusting Him, down we go.

We will not go into the wilderness of doubt and fear when we, "*Taste and see that the Lord is good. Oh, the joys of those who take refuge in him*" (Psalm 34:8, NLT). God asks us to try Him so He can show us how totally trustworthy He is. He loves His children and will never lead us down the wrong path. It's because of His grace towards us that we are carried to the place of complete trust in Him.

---

[4] *Life Application Study Bible, NLT* (Wheaton, IL: Tyndale House Publishers, Inc., 1996), 219.

Day Seventeen

GOD'S GRACE

As I started this page, I wondered if I'd be able to explain God's grace. Could there be words in existence that fully explain it? The Scriptures are full of the words, "God's grace," and hopefully I can share the magnificence of those words. In my research I found words like: unmerited favor, love, devotion, forgiveness, mercy, pardon, and spiritual blessing. But what does that mean for us? "*God saved you by His grace when you believed. And you can't take credit for this; it is a gift from God*" (Ephesians 2:8, NLT).

"*For if you are trying to make yourselves right with God by keeping the law, you have been cut off from Christ! You have fallen away from God's grace*" (Galatians 5:4, NLT). The law alone couldn't save us; only Jesus giving His life for us because of His love could save us. We can't earn God's favor by being good enough. Only through His life and the cross could His grace be revealed to us. We can't take any credit for our salvation, because it's a free gift from God.

"*For He made Him who knew no sin to be sin for us, that we might become the righteousness of God in Him*" (2 Corinthians 5:21, NKJV). On the cross Jesus gave us His righteousness, grace, and holiness for our sins. A huge difference in value—He took the agony of the cross and gave us freedom from sin.

Paul says: *"It is he who saved us and chose us for his holy work not because we deserved it but because that was His plan long before the world began—to show his love and kindness to us through Christ"* (2 Timothy 1:9, TLB); *"But whatever I am now it is all because God poured out such kindness and grace on me—and not without results ..."* (1 Corinthians 15:10a, NLT). Sometimes when I hear a special song that touches my spirit I shake inside, because I am so thankful that I gave my heart to the Lord so many years ago. The Lord redeemed me—bought me with His blood and removed sin's grip on my life. I was undeserving of His favor, undeserving of His blessings, and undeserving of His mercy. When He stepped into my life, it was the start of a journey of change and learning what He had for me to do. I have complete freedom in Him.

"For out of His fullness [the superabundance of His grace and truth] we have all received grace upon grace [spiritual blessing upon spiritual blessing, favor upon favor, and gift heaped upon gift]" (John 1:16, AMP); *"May God give you more and more grace and peace as you grow in your knowledge of God and Jesus our Lord"* (2 Peter 1:2, NLT). The gift of God's grace gives us undeserved love, peace, hope, and joy.

Day Eighteen

JOY

King David became proud of himself, and that angered God; however, God was faithful to David and restored him:

For his [God's] anger lasts only a moment, but his favor lasts a lifetime! Weeping may last through the night, but joy comes with the morning ... You have turned my mourning into joyful dancing. You have taken away my clothes of mourning and clothed me with joy, that I might sing praises to You ... I will give You thanks forever! (Psalm 30:5, 11–12, NLT)

The end of my marriage devastated me. Sometimes I cried most of the day and night, and I can't count the number of times I cried myself to sleep. Thankfully the Lord restores. Tears dry up, and grief ends. I can honestly say that one morning the joy of the Lord was restored in my spirit, and He blessed me with peace and contentment. I along with King David rejoiced because God did restore me to Himself, and I too am thankful.

The disciples questioned Jesus when He was trying to explain to them what was going to happen to Him:

I go to the Father and you shall see me no more … The world will greatly rejoice over what is going to happen to me, and you will weep. But your weeping shall suddenly be turned to wonderful joy when you see Me again. It will be the same joy as that of a woman in labor when her child is born—her anguish gives way to rapturous joy … (John 16:10, 20–21, TLB)

When a mother sees her newborn baby for the first time, she is full of joy. She lovingly holds her baby in her arms and checks its fingers and toes and is amazed by their perfection. When God looks at His children, He too holds us in His loving arms and checks our fingers and toes, so to speak. Do we bring Him rapturous joy? Are we obedient to His plans for us? Do we make Him smile when we honor His name?

We bring joy to God when we are born into His kingdom, but God's greatest joy is in His Son, Jesus. Jesus totally surrendered Himself to His Father and was obedient to death on a cross. God's plan was fulfilled in Him.

Jesus experienced joy because He was obedient to God His Father and willingly gave His life for our salvation. Jesus wants us to be obedient to God and to follow His plans for our lives. King David found that joy: "*I take joy in doing your will, my God …*" (Psalm 40:8a, NLT).

If we have a right relationship with the Lord, which includes being faithful in obedience and a willingness to seek Him in all things, we will have God's joy in our spirits.

Day Nineteen

WHAT'S THE PLAN?

David wrote: "*The Lord will work out his plans for my life—for your faithful love, O Lord, endures forever. Don't abandon me, for you made me*" (Psalm 138:8, NLT). I keep a daily planner and record plans for the month. When the month is over and I look back, I see many changes of plans. Some plans were totally scrapped and some new ones were added. As the saying goes, "It's not written in stone." When reviewing, I wonder if I asked the Lord if the plans made by me were what He wanted me to do. When I did invite God into my plans but unexpected events and tragedies occurred and I felt abandoned by God, I had to remember that God's plans are perfect and never change … like mine do. He loves me, and His plans give me hope and a future: "'*For I know the plans I have for you,*' declares the Lord, '*plans to prosper you and not to harm you, plans to give you hope and a future*'" (Jeremiah 29:11). I don't need to understand His plans for me, I just have to trust Him. God is in control. "*Many are the plans in a person's heart, but it is the Lord's purpose [plan] that prevails*" (Proverbs 19:21). Stay in His plan. It is good.

Look here, you who say, "Today or tomorrow we are going to a certain town and will stay there a year" … How do you know what your life will be like tomorrow? Your life is like the morning fog—it's here a little while, then it's gone. What you ought to say is, "If the Lord wants us to, we will live and do this and that"… Remember, it is a sin to know what you ought to do and then not do it. (James 4:13–17, NLT)

My sister Irene loved the Lord and was called by Him to be a missionary nurse to northern Alberta. She said no to the Lord and during her lifetime made other wrong choices that at times left her life in pieces. Many good things happened to her too, but at times she wondered what her life would have been like had she followed the Lord's plan.

"Jesus gave his life for our sins, just as God our Father planned, in order to rescue us from this evil world in which we live" (Galatians 1:4, NLT). Think of the magnitude of God's plan for His Son, Jesus. God had that plan from the very beginning of time to bring glory to Himself and His only Son. The cross didn't happen by chance! It wasn't a mistake! It was God's plan.

Day Twenty

JOYFUL AND THANKFUL IN HIS WILL

False doctrine was being taught in the Colossian church. They were being told that they could know God's will through knowledge alone. In his letter to the Colossians, Paul instructs them to learn the Christian way of understanding God's will. We are to pray and ask God "… *to give you complete knowledge of his will and to give you spiritual wisdom and understanding*" (Colossians 1:9, NLT). God's will is His plan for us, and He wants us to understand His plan.

After we submit to God's will, our lives will "*honor and please the Lord*," and as our lives "*produce every kind of good fruit*," we will "*learn to know God better and better*" (Colossians 1:10, NLT). Walk deeper with Him!

Paul also "*pray*(s) *that you will be strengthened with all his glorious power*," and for the "*endurance and patience you need*" and to be "*filled with joy, always thanking the Father*" (Colossians 1:11, NLT).

In Colossians 1:12 (NLT), Paul says to be "*always thanking the Father*" to God for all things, because He has "*enabled*" us to "*share in the inheritance that belongs to his people*," and to live in "*the light*" of His salvation. How great is the inheritance of sins forgiven and living with the Lord!

I have been a Christian for many years, and sometimes I still struggle with knowing the Lord's will. I wonder if it's because I really don't want to do what He asks. Some things He asks seem too difficult, and I struggle with obedience. What if I'm asked to forgive someone who really doesn't deserve it? Sometimes I feel like I'm not equipped to do His will. Am I smart enough emotionally, or spiritually strong enough, to help others? Can I be joyful and thankful?

But when I pray for the assurance of His presence and study His Word in a deep and meaningful way, when my "roots go down deep" in Him, I know for sure that I can do what He asks. The better I know Him, the easier it is to do good things for others. Jesus sent the Holy Spirit to help us do what we need to do—to bring Him glory. I believe in His guidance. I study His Word and pray. He blesses me with the inheritance of heaven when I walk in close communion with Him. I trust in what He asks me to do, and when I surrender my will to Him, He is honored.

Day Twenty-One
ROOTS GO DOWN DEEP

*"May your roots go down deep into the soil of God's
marvellous love; and may you be able to feel and
understand … how long, how wide, how deep,
and how high his love really is …"*
(Ephesians 3:17b–18, TLB)

Everything planted in the ground has a root system. Our root system is nourished by the tree of life, the Lord.

Just being a Christian isn't enough to nourish us through life and what it throws at us. Just going to church isn't enough, and life's pleasures aren't enough. We need a deep thirst for a relationship with the Lord. Our roots need to go deep into Him through meditating on His Word: *"Turn my eyes from worthless things, and give me life through your word,"* (Psalm 119:37, NLT).

In Luke 8:13, Jesus tells the parable of the sower: *"Those [seeds] on the rocky soil are those who, when they hear, receive the word with joy; and these have no firm root; they believe for a while, and in time of temptation fall away"* (NASB). We cannot live a shallow Christian life and flourish; we need to go deep.

I conducted some research on Google to study the root systems of trees. The roots of many trees are shallow and only go down twelve to thirty-six inches and then spread out to find moisture. The mighty oak tree, however, is a different story. It sends out a main root called the "taproot" that can go down twenty feet to find moisture and then spreads out horizontally. The oldest known tree is a redwood called "Eternal God." It has a root depth of four hundred feet. This tree is the perfect example of how our walk with the Lord should be—deep, deep down in His love. When our roots go down deep, we tap into the "taproot" and are nourished spiritually: "*But if some of the branches* [Jews] *were broken off, and you* [Gentiles], *being a wild olive, were grafted in among them and became partaker with them of the rich root of the olive tree*" (Romans 11:17, NASB). Jesus is the root. Rooted in the loving, merciful, compassionate God, we can find living water in Him that will keep us strong and help us endure whatever comes our way.

> *"I, Jesus, have sent my My angel to testify to you these things ... I am the Root and the Offspring of David, the Bright and Morning Star." And the Spirit and the Bride say, "Come!...And let him who thirsts come. Whoever desires, let him take the water of life freely.* (Revelation 22:16–17, NKJV)

Day Twenty-Two

THE HEART OF THE WALK

Visualize walking with the Lord this way: A little girl, four or five, wanting to walk with her daddy, puts her right foot on the toes of his left foot and then puts her left foot on the toes of his right foot. Daddy starts walking, and she is in perfect step with him as she giggles happily. We need to do the same with our Heavenly Father so we can be in perfect step with Him. God will never take us where we shouldn't go.

We live in an age where we see many walking away from the Lord. They are Christians, but aren't rooted in Him through His Word. "*As you therefore have received Christ Jesus the Lord, so walk in Him, rooted and built up in Him and established in the faith …*" (Colossians 2:6–7a, NKJV). The only way to survive the brokenness of this world is to walk solidly with Him. He will carry us to healing.

When admonishing some Pharisees one day, Jesus quoted one of the prophesies of Isaiah "*These people honor me with their lips, but their hearts are far from me*" (Matthew 15:8, NLT). I once heard a story of a lady and her dog. She was outside working in her yard, her dog by her side. The dog heard leaves rustling in a tree, where she spotted a bird. She kept barking and circling the tree until the lady called her back to her side. The dog wouldn't look at her but kept its eyes on the tree and the bird. Her dog was beside her, but its desires were on the bird in the tree. Sometimes that's the way we walk with the Lord. We walk with Him, but our heart is elsewhere, like with our spouse, our children, our jobs or finances, or other concerns. The answer is to focus on Jesus alone and make Him the center of our attention, dependant on Him for each step.

"*Try always to be led along together by the Holy Spirit* ..." (Ephesians 4:3a, TLB). As the Holy Spirit walks with us and leads us, we have to be willing to be in step with Him and to focus on Him and trust His leading. He will choose the right path for us. The Lord doesn't get lost or need a map for directions; He knows the way. Walking out of step with Him can be difficult. If we lag behind we can lose sight of Him and get lost. If we walk too far ahead, we won't know when He makes a turn, and we'll get lost. So let's get back in step with Him, put our two feet on His, and walk where He leads—happily, like the little girl.

Day Twenty-Three
CRACKED POT: BROKEN VESSEL

*"… Lord, you are our Father. We are the clay, and you
are the Potter. We are all formed by your hand."*
(Isaiah 64:8, NLT)

We were formed from dirt by God and that if we stay in close communion with Him, we will not end up a cracked pot that leaks away our closeness with Him, or a broken vessel that has lost all intimacy. We need to let God take us, a lump of clay, and make us into a beautiful piece of pottery.

I volunteer at our local soup kitchen and at times I'm asked to bake cookies. I have a favorite mixing bowl, and the last time I used it I noticed that the wet ingredients were streaming out of a long crack on the side. So … it had to be thrown out. When we as Spirit-filled Christians have a crack, we leak away the power of the Holy Spirit. Unless we are remade, we're of no more use.

*But in a great house there are not only vessels of gold and silver,
but also of wood and clay, some for honor and some for dishonor.
Therefore, if anyone cleanses himself from the latter, he will be a
vessel of honor …* (2 Timothy 2:20–21a, NKJV)

Under normal circumstances, a gold or silver pot can't be cracked or broken. It stays true to the one who created it; however, wood can be shattered and clay can be cracked. Let us, God's creation, be made of gold or silver so we can stay faithful and be used by the Lord for His works. Make me a vessel of honor to the Lord.

Make-over programs are very popular on television these days, and they make-over everything from hair and make-up, to wardrobes, landscapes, and homes. Jeremiah writes about a potter's make-over of clay: *"But the jar he was making did not turn out as he had hoped, so he crushed it into a lump of clay again and started over"* (Jeremiah 18:4, NLT). God created us out of clay, and just like the potter mentioned here, God through the cross remakes us into what He planned for us to be. The touch of our Maker can restore, renew, and remake.

Day Twenty-Four

CRUSHED AND BROKEN IN SPIRIT

King David said, "*The Lord is close to the broken hearted and saves those who are crushed in spirit*" (Psalms 34:18). David was familiar with heartache, but he also knew who could mend his heart: "*Praise the Lord. How good it is to sing praises to our God … He heals the broken hearted and binds up their wounds*" (Psalms 147:1, 3). King David was broken-hearted over many things. He grieved over the sins he had committed, the betrayal of family and friends, the deaths of loved ones, and at times he felt rejected by God; however, these psalms end in praise, worship, and thankfulness to the God he loved.

Sometimes we wonder why God allows such brokenness in our lives, but through Paul He tells us plainly that he is a:

… wonderful God … the source of every mercy…who … comforts and strengthens us in our hardships and trials. And why does He do this? So that when others are troubled, needing our sympathy and encouragement, we can pass on to them the same help and comfort God has given us. (2 Corinthians 1:3–4, TLB)

There is a trend today called "pay it forward." In a lineup someone buys a coffee and also pays for a coffee for the next person in line. It's a blessing for sure. In Paul's letter to the Corinthians, he tells them that when the Lord helps us in times of sorrow, we can "pay it forward" and encourage others. Instead of giving up and flying away to another planet, we can let the Lord unpack our bags of brokenness and let the Holy Spirit in so He can heal our hearts.

In his letter to the Thessalonians, Paul tells us to stand strong against heartache, because God will mend our broken hearts when we allow Him to work in us:

> ... may our Lord Jesus Christ himself and God our Father, who loved us and by his grace gave us eternal comfort and a wonderful hope, comfort you and strengthen you in every good thing you do and say (2 Thessalonians 2:16–17, NLT).

Day Twenty-Five

THROUGH

Yet again I heard of another couple separating. It seems to be the new normal in our society, and it brings hurt into my heart for them. Betrayal is as old as history itself, but when it affects us personally, it can destroy us. With the Lord's help, we can take a journey from heartbreak to restoration.

Isaiah declares God's words to the Israelites, but it's a promise to all who believe:

When you go through deep waters and great trouble, I will be with you. When you go through rivers of difficulty, you will not drown! When you walk through the fire of oppression, you will not be burned up–the flames will not consume you. For I am the Lord your God … (Isaiah 43:2–3a, TLB)

We should never try to go through any difficulties alone, because when God puts His name behind a promise, we will not drown or burn up in our pain.

"I can do all things through Christ who strengthens me," (Philippians 4:13, NKJV). The "all things" here for me would be survival. We can survive because the Lord gives us strength to walk, talk, breathe, and keep above our sorrow. *"And let the peace that comes from Christ rule in your hearts ... And always be thankful"* (Colossians 3:15, NLT). It's fair to ask the question, "How can I possibly have peace in my heart when I'm dying inside?" God's peace has nothing to do with our feelings. It's His presence in our soul saying, "It's okay. I'm here. You will survive; just cling to me and I will carry you through." God didn't plan for marriages to end, but when they do, He can and will take us to the other side of sorrow. I can also hear you saying, "Be thankful? Are you out of your mind?" We aren't thankful for betrayal. We aren't thankful that we're in so much emotional pain that, at times, we don't want to live, but we can be thankful that the Lord loves us enough to go through each trial with us. We can also be thankful for family and friends who come alongside us, pray for us, and love us as we heal.

King David's psalms are a perfect model for healing: from pain to praise to thankfulness. Through many of his troubles, he felt like there was no hope, that all was lost; however, he always ended up looking for good things to dwell on. He was a man of music and wrote many praise psalms. His music calmed King Saul's tormented spirit as he played for him, and music can speak to our souls too.

Day Twenty-Six

THROUGH (PART TWO)

Christian writer Amy Peterson states that singing releases hormones in our brain that relieve stress, and when we sing together, our hearts beat as one.[5] The power of gospel music healed King David's heartaches and will heal us too. Sing praises to the Lord and let Him heal you.

A Christian friend whose marriage ended after many years, and like me was devastated, asked me how I survived. I told him, "The truth is, I was on my face before the Lord. Sometimes it was every minute, sometimes every hour, and after many months of crying and praying before the Lord and studying His 'Love Letter' to me (the Bible), emotional healing came."

When we get up in the morning and nothing has changed—we're still broken and it seems like there's no hope that we'll ever be whole again—that's the time to grab hold of Jesus' nail-pierced hand and praise and thank Him for all He has done for us. We need to believe He loves us and just live one day at a time. Remember, when we're down, that's

---

[5] Amy Peterson, "A Reason to Sing," *Our Daily Bread,* June 9, 2017.

the time the devil will try to completely destroy us and our love for God. Think on good things!

I end this page with a prayer that I wrote in my journal early on in my journey: "Please don't leave me, Lord. I can't make it without You. Each day as I come to You, please give me the strength to carry on. This is a tough thing that You allowed, Lord, but I thank You for helping me get through it. When I study Your Word and talk with You and listen to what You have to say to me, I can exchange all my fears, tears, and pain for Your strength and power. I come to You emotionally drained and physically exhausted, and as I learn to be thankful in spite of my pain and sing praises to You again, then I will survive. As you said so many times in Your Word, 'Let's go to the other side!'"

Day Twenty-Seven

"Let's Go to the Other Side"

Often in the Gospels Jesus said to His disciples, "Let's go to the other side." For me that meant untying the boat from the dock and going to the other side of my pain so that when I got there and got out of the boat, my healing would be complete. I was healed from the storm of a broken marriage but got right back into the boat and ran into a storm called cancer. Like the disciples, I was afraid. I didn't want to get in the boat again. I wanted to stay docked so that maybe the storm would pass by.

"*Then Jesus said, 'Let's go off by ourselves to a quiet place and rest awhile*" (Mark 6:31, NLT). Many followed by land, and Jesus fed five thousand with five loaves and two fish. "*Immediately after this, Jesus insisted that His disciples get back into the boat and head across the lake ... he went up into the hills by himself to pray*" (Mark 6:45–46). They went back and forth across the Sea of Galilee many times in the three years of Jesus' ministry.

One time Jesus and His disciples sailed across the lake from Galilee and healed a demon possessed man. When the man wanted to go back with Jesus, He told him to stay there and tell others what had happened, and a church was planted (Luke 8:26–39, NLT).

Another time Jesus said to His disciples, *"Let's cross over to the other side of the lake"* (Luke 8:22, NLT). They left and a storm came up. Jesus was at the back of the boat taking a nap, and when Jesus rebuked the wind, the storm stopped.

Today when we get into a boat we're required to wear a life jacket to keep us from drowning. The disciples' life jacket was Jesus. If they'd believed that, they never would have been terrified of the storms. No drowning with Him on board! We probably won't arrive on the other side immediately, as they did, but as long as Jesus is with us, we should have no fear. He will get us to the other side of our pain. I read somewhere that "we should chart our course in pencil and let God have the eraser." God's course is written in ink. Jesus wasn't afraid of the storms or waves—He just walked on them!

Day Twenty-Eight

KEEP YOUR THOUGHTS CAPTIVE

From time to time we have bad attitudes that we need to clean up and turn into positives; however, it's not only attitudes that need to be taken captive, but our sinful thoughts, desires, and actions need to be put under the Holy Spirit's control. We tend to jump into action when a new thought or activity comes before us. Often we don't think about the consequences and inevitably get into trouble. We're accountable for all we think, say, and do. If we focus on the Lord and the power of the cross, we won't fall to our wrong thoughts. God's thoughts are written in the Bible, and He lays down the rules in Scripture for us to be victorious in our thinking. Jesus says here: "*If you abide in My word, you are My disciples indeed. And you shall know the truth, and the truth shall make you free*" (John 8:31–32, NKJV). We don't need to be in the bondage of sin that starts with uncontrolled thoughts that are contrary to God's Word. We can overcome.

"*The weapons we use in our fight are not the world's weapons but God's powerful weapons, which we use to destroy strongholds*" (2 Corinthians 10:4, GNT). A spiritual war is being waged for our thoughts, actions, and even our imaginations. The devil wants to destroy us and can use our minds to do that, if we let him. The Lord defeated the devil on the cross, so it makes perfect sense to me to go with the winner who will keep our thoughts captive and make them pure and holy.

Wherever my thoughts go, good or bad, they are in my mind until I either accept them as good or throw them out because they are not good to pursue and can lead to sin.

Paul wrote to the Philippians: "... *Fix your thoughts on what is true, and honorable, and right, and pure, and lovely and admirable. Think about things that are excellent and worthy of praise*" (Philippians 4:8, NLT). And I say, "Amen."

Day Twenty-Nine

I Will Serve You

We as believers are called to serve the Lord and others. Our service to the Lord is to be obedient to Him and do what He asks of us. We are also called by the Lord to serve Him by telling others about His love for us. After we serve the Lord first, we are called to serve others in our churches and our communities.

Paul was an unwavering servant of Jesus. He began each letter he wrote by identifying whom he was serving, and he stated that it was because of God's will: "*Paul, a servant of Christ Jesus …*" (Romans 1:1); "*Paul, a servant of God …*" (Titus 1:1). He began all the letters to the churches by confirming that he was "an apostle of Jesus by the Lord's will." Paul's primary goal was to win souls to the Lord. He never forgot whom he served.

"*Has the Lord redeemed you? Then speak out! Tell others He has saved you …*" (Psalm 107:2a, TLB). Although methods are different today, God still gives us the words to say as we share Him and the message of the cross with others. I believe that God uses our circumstances, personalities, and abilities to perform specific service to and for Him. We're all wired differently.

We're called to serve in our churches. We don't have to be pastors or trustees to serve; we can lead a small group or drive a senior to an appointment or for medication. We can take time to babysit for a frazzled mom so she can go out for coffee or shop for groceries in peace. We're also called to serve in our communities. We can volunteer at local seniors' centers, soup kitchens, or hospitals. God called us to serve and be gracious.

"As a face is reflected in water, so the heart reflects the real person" (Proverbs 27:19, NLT). I worked as a server in a seniors' complex and tried to make each individual feel special. One day after I served lunch, a lady by the name of Doris spoke with me and said that she saw such peace in me that she told her friend she thought I was a Christian. I was blessed. God calls us to share about His Son, Jesus, by example, by serving, and by encouraging.

To Be Pure and Holy

"God has united you with Christ Jesus ... Christ made
us right with God; he made us pure and holy,
and he freed us from sin."
(1 Corinthians 1:30, NLT)

Being holy isn't something the Lord put in us—it is Jesus Himself living in us. In the sermon on the mount, Jesus said, *"Blessed are the pure in heart, for they will see God"* (Matthew 5:8). Purity comes when we are in complete harmony with God, a likeness of Him.

When we see children who look like their parents, we often say that they are the "spitting image" of either the mom or the dad. When others see us, can they say that we're the "spitting image" of our Heavenly Father, holy and pure?

Paul's goal was to do all, and be all, for the Lord. *"Not that I have already attained, or am already perfected; but I press on, that I may lay hold of that for which Christ Jesus has also laid hold of me"* (Philippians 3:12, NKJV). We look at ourselves and wonder if we'll ever become perfect, but that thought comes from the human perspective. Perfection from the Lord's point of view is what He sees in our heart. Millie Stamm writes:

> ...when we receive Jesus Christ as our Lord and Saviour, our hearts are made pure through the cleansing power of His blood.

The pure in heart are not pious, nor hypocritical. They are not perfect, but sincere and honest, genuine and real. Their motives, desires, and intentions are pure. They are submissive to God's will.[6]

"Now may the God of peace make you holy in every way, and may your whole spirit and soul and body be kept blameless until our Lord Jesus Christ comes again" (Thessalonians 5:23, NLT). Becoming holy means to think less of what the world has to offer and more about how the Lord wants us to live. It needs to be the Lord first, with our will and rights bringing up the rear.

John the Baptist's disciples were upset because people were following Jesus instead of John. John, however, knew that Jesus was the Messiah and that he was the one who came to prepare the way for Jesus: *"He* [Jesus] *must increase, but I must decrease"* (John 3:30, NKJV). That is the perfect example of how we need to live. We can become like Him, holy and pure, as we walk in the light of His love.

---

[6] Millie Stamm, *Be Still and Know* (Grand Rapids, MI: Daybreak Books, Zondervan Publishing House, 1978), July 24.

Day Thirty-One
DARKNESS TO LIGHT

Jesus replied, "My light will shine for you just a little
longer. Walk in the light while you can, so the darkness
will not overtake you. Those who walk in the darkness
cannot see where they are going. Put your trust
in the light while there is still time; then you
will become children of the light."
(John 12:35–36, NLT)

Jesus knew His life on earth was coming to an end, but He also knew He would rise again and be our light for all eternity if we accepted His free gift of salvation.

Some winters ago, we experienced many cold, cloudy, and dreary months. One such morning in early spring as I was doing my devotions, the sun broke through the clouds. As it shone in on me, I could feel its warmth. This is a perfect example of what Jesus, the light of the world, does to the condition of our spiritual hearts if we ask Him to dispel the darkness. Parts of a poem from my book, *Two Alone*, read:

SEASONS OF THE SOUL:
The soul that is lost is like a winter's night, cold, dark and despairing. No hope of new creation, no faith for the future, nothing to anticipate. Oh, what agony. Oh, what heartache.

What a barren land of wasted life. An eternity of darkness. But wait! What is this occurrence? "The Resurrection?" What does this mean? Could there be hope? Is there a chance? Oh! The darkness is lifting. The warmth is replacing the cold. Glorious sunshine is flooding the soul … radiant beams of the summer sunshine illuminate the soul. Amazing! The soul is alive …"[7]

Jesus is the light. He alone can bring light to the darkness of our souls. His light drives the darkness out and gives us His purity and holiness. *"But you are a chosen people, a royal priesthood, a holy nation, God's special possession, that you may declare the praises of Him who called you out of darkness into His wonderful light"* (1 Peter 2:9). Peter is addressing the Jews here, but because God extended His plan of salvation to the Gentiles, we are included in becoming the children of the light.

---

[7] Darlene Rose Busse, *Two Alone* (Baltimore, MD: America House Book Publishers, 2000), 199–200.

Day Thirty-Two
DARKNESS TO LIGHT (PART TWO)

*"I [Jesus] have come as a Light to shine in this dark
world, so that all who put their trust in me will no
longer wander in the darkness."*
(John 12:46, TLB)

Sometimes when life happens we quit trusting God, and our souls
become dark. Depression, sadness, and anger can overtake us, but
just as the sun rises in the east each day, so the Son of God can lift us up
into Him again.

Jesus was teaching the crowds and said to them, *"You are the light of
the world—like a city on a hilltop that cannot be hidden"* (Matthew 5:14,
NLT); *"No one lights a lamp and hides it in a jar or puts it under a bed.
Instead, they put it on a stand, so that those who come in can see the light"*
(Luke 8:16).

The power went off in my whole area in the middle of the night,
and extreme quiet and darkness woke me up. The darkness felt so thick,
I could cut it with a knife. I felt my way to a candle, lit it, and put it
on the nightstand beside my bed. That little candle lit up the whole
bedroom. As I was lying there thinking and praying, I thought about
Jesus as He walked here on earth. He often slept on the Mount of Olives
with no electricity and no candle, but He was never overwhelmed by the
darkness. Eventually I realized that it wasn't dark for Him, because He

was the light. Because His love penetrates all that I am and all that I do, I can give Him all my fears and walk with Him. His light overtakes my darkness.

"… *God is light; in him there is no darkness at all*" (1 John 1:5b, NLT). We are lying if we say we have fellowship with God but go on living in spiritual darkness. Paul says:

> *For once you were full of darkness, but now you have light from the Lord. So live as people of light! For this light within you produces only what is good and right and true. Carefully determine what pleases the Lord. Take no part in the worthless deeds of evil and darkness …* (Ephesians 5:8–11a, NLT)

God wants us to be an example of the light so others can see Him in us.

Day Thirty-Three

WHAT DO YOU SEE?

"You are so proud of knowing God's laws, but you dishonor Him by breaking them. No wonder the Scriptures say that the world speaks evil of God because of you."
(Romans 2:23–24, TLB)

A few years ago, I worked in ladies' wear at a local department store. One Sunday a clerk from the hardware department came to us with some articles of clothing. She had a customer who insisted that the clothes were on for 35 percent off. As suspected, they weren't on sale. Without missing a beat, the clerk from hardware spouted, "She probably just came from church." It's really too bad that we as Christians have a reputation as thieves. Is that a reflection of God? *"For from the very beginning, God decided that those that came to Him ... should become like His Son ..."* (Romans 8:29, TLB).

I read of a Christian man who was being abused with unkind words by a supervisor at his workplace. What made it worse was that it happened in front of his co-workers. The man could have retaliated, but instead he prayed for his supervisor. I don't know the outcome, but I do know that he did what Jesus would have done.

"... don't let this bad example influence you. Follow only what is good. Remember that those who do good prove that they are God's children, and

those who do evil prove that they do not know God" (3 John 1:11, NLT). A television commercial shows a lady running from a store with a bag of merchandise in one hand and the receipt in the other. Suddenly she starts yelling loudly to her husband, "Start the car; start the car." You know she's trying to get away with something that isn't right. Then there are people who go back to a store to tell the clerk that she missed charging them for an item, and they pay for it. Some people go back into a store to give back the extra money they were given by mistake. Which of these examples show what Jesus would do? Let's show a difference in the way we act. Maybe that difference will help someone find the Lord.

Day Thirty-Four
Written by God

I've heard people say that they don't like to read the Old Testament because the genealogies are boring and there are too many wars and too much bloodshed. In reality, the genealogy is traced from Adam to Noah on to King David and to Jesus. The wars weren't waged because God was cruel or bloodthirsty but because the Israelites, God's chosen race, were disobedient and worshiped other gods.

"You show that you are a letter from Christ … written not with ink but with the Spirit of the living God, not on tablets of stone but on tablets of human hearts" (2 Corinthians 3:3). If we mirror ourselves after God and His Word, we can overcome all things and become like Him. His written letter to us shows us how to live victoriously in Him. We need to ask ourselves: Do our lives mirror God, our personal Author and Creator? If someone reads our lives, can they see Jesus? As we grow spiritually, we need to learn how to meditate on the truths of the Bible by reading and studying each chapter and verse.

The Bible introduces us to God the Father, God the Son, and God the Holy Spirit. It gives us a picture of the Trinity and teaches us how to live in harmony with them. It's a history book and a love letter, and it reveals the events of ages past, as well as what heaven is like and what will happen in the future.

We can learn from God's Word how to maneuver through life from heartache to restoration by studying the Bible, learning who God really is, and becoming intimate with Jesus as we rely on the Holy Spirit for guidance and use the gifts God has given us to be the image of Him.

Day Thirty-Five

GOD'S NATURE

Let's look deeper into God's divine nature. There is so much more! God is trustworthy:

"Lean on, trust in, and be confident in the Lord with all your heart and mind and do not rely on your own insight or understanding. In all your ways know, recognize, and acknowledge Him and He will direct and make straight and plain your paths." (Proverbs 3:5-6, TAB)

When we ask God to guide us in a situation or help us make right decisions, we can trust that He will direct us correctly. He knows what's best for us.

God is security: *"The name of the Lord is a strong tower; the righteous run to it and are safe"* (Proverbs 18:10, NKJV). When life challenges are frightening or can harm us, we can run to God and be safe. The President of the United States is driven around in a car with eight-inch-thick walls. He is safe; we are safe in the Lord.

King David outlined God's characteristics:

He forgives all my sins and heals all my diseases. He redeems me from death and crowns me with love and tender mercies. He fills my life with good things. My youth is renewed like the eagle's! The Lord gives righteousness and justice to all who are treated unfairly. The Lord is compassionate and merciful, slow to get angry. (Psalm 103:3–8a, NLT)

He desires our praise. The angels praise Him, as does all of creation (Psalm 103:21–22). We can see the Lord in every area of our lives, and we need to praise and worship Him.

God sees everything. "*Nothing in all creation is hidden from God's sight. Everything is uncovered and laid bare before the eyes of Him to whom we must give account*" (Hebrews 4:13). In today's world, we find surveillance cameras on almost every street corner, in businesses, and in homes. Much is captured on film or video. God, however, sees all things within and without, without cameras. We need have no fear. God will watch over us if we love and trust Him.

God is a compassionate comforter:

Praise be to the God and Father of our Lord Jesus Christ, the Father of compassion and the God of all comfort, who comforts us in all our troubles, so that we can comfort those in any trouble with the comfort we ourselves have received from God. (2 Corinthians 1:3–4)

God wants us to reciprocate His passion and comfort to others who need strength and encouragement. God does care about us.

Day Thirty-Six

THE CONSUMING FIRE

*Now Moses was tending the flock ... and came to Horeb
[Sinai], the mountain of God. There the angel of the
Lord appeared to him in flames of fire from within a
bush ... though the bush was on fire it did not burn up.
So Moses thought, "I will go over and see this strange
sight" ... When the Lord saw that he had gone over to
look, God called to him from within the bush, "Moses!
Moses!" And Moses said, "Here I am." "Do not come any
closer," God said. "Take off your sandals, for the place
where you are standing is holy ground" ... At this, Moses
hid his face, because he was afraid to look at God.*
(Exodus 3:1–6)

Today would we take off our shoes in respect for God? Would we
cover our faces in reverent fear? Have we become too casual towards
Him in our modern society to worship Him with honor?

Moses reminded the Israelites of all that God had done for them,
including giving them the Ten Commandments. "*You stood at the foot of
the mountain [Sinai], and the mountain burned with fire; flames shot far
into the sky ... And the Lord spoke to you from the fire; you heard His words
but didn't see Him*" (Deuteronomy 4:11–12, TLB); "*For the Lord your
God is a consuming fire ...*" (Deuteronomy 4:24a); "*The earth trembles*

at his glance; the mountains burst into flame at his touch" (Psalm 104:32, TLB). The province of British Columbia has many mountains, and because the summer has been extremely dry this year, the mountains are indeed on fire … and I wonder if God "glanced" at them. "… *The breath of the Lord, like fire from a volcano, will set it ablaze*" (Isaiah 30:33b, NLT). We are seeing an increase in volcanic eruptions, and I wonder …

> *"Once again I will shake not only the earth but the heavens also."* *This means that all of creation will be shaken and removed, so that only unshakeable things will remain. Since we are receiving a Kingdom that is unshakeable, let us be thankful and please God by worshiping Him with holy fear and awe. For our God is a devouring fire.* (Hebrews 12:26b–29, NLT)

A few years ago there was an earthquake in Nepal that actually shook Mount Everest … and I wonder.

God's consuming fire can be what we call His "refining" fire, like a chunk of coal. Because of the earth's heat and pressure, the coal emerges as a diamond. When God's refining fire is on us, we can either burn, die, or be tested under pressure and come out a precious gem in God's sight.

Day Thirty-Seven

GOD PROVIDES

God told Abraham to go up on the mountain and sacrifice his son, Isaac. When Isaac asked where the sacrificial lamb was, Abraham said: "*God will provide a sheep for the burnt offering, my son ...*" (Genesis 22:8, NLT). Abraham was about to kill his son when the Lord intervened. "*Then Abraham looked up and saw a ram caught by its horns in a thicket*" (Genesis 22:13a, NLT). Abraham named the place "*the Lord will provide*" (Genesis 22:14a, NLT).

King David writes that God provides food for our tables: "*You take care of the earth and water it, making it rich and fertile. The river of God has plenty of water; it provides a bountiful harvest of grain, for you have ordered it so*" (Psalm 65:9, NLT).

Paul talks about giving the gift of money to those in need. We are called to provide financial help to the needy: "*And God will generously provide all you need. Then you will always have everything you need and plenty left over to share with others*" (2 Corinthians 9:8, NLT). God blesses willing givers.

"*Jesus went throughout Galilee, teaching in their synagogues, proclaiming the good news of the kingdom, and healing every disease and sickness among them*" (Matthew 4:23). Jesus provided the way for us to have spiritual and physical healing. He showed us the way to heaven through Him.

"*And my God will supply all your needs according to His riches in glory in Christ Jesus*" (Philippians 4:19, NASB). We can't out-give God! I recognize the things the Lord has provided for me, and I'm thankful for all things, good and bad. I'm not saying I love and appreciate the bad things in my life, but I'm so thankful that God, the provider, carried me through the tough times. He only wants good for us.

There are two versions of Proverbs 16:33 that I'd like to leave with you that show us that God is totally in control: "*The lot is cast into the lap, but its every decision is from the Lord*" (AMP); "*We may throw the dice, but the Lord determines how they fall*" (NLT).

Day Thirty-Eight
HEDGE OF PROTECTION

*The Lord is my rock, my fortress, and my savior; my God
is my rock, in whom I find protection. He is my shield,
the power that saves me, and my place of safety. I called
on the Lord, who is worthy of praise,
and he saved me from my enemies.*
(Psalm 18:2–3, NLT)

God's protection of His people is limitless and can take many
forms. David characterized God's care with five military symbols.
God is like—a rock that can't be moved by any who would
harm us—a fortress or place of safety where the enemy can't
follow—a shield that comes between us and harm—strength
of salvation, a symbol of might and power—a stronghold high
above our enemies. If you need protection, look to God.[8]

Isaiah uses the example of God's vineyard of Jerusalem and Judah
(the Israelites) and what would happen to them if they turned their
hearts away from Him. He did place a hedge of protection around them,
but they kept turning away from Him, so He told them the outcome:
"*Now I will tell you what I am going to do to my vineyard: I will take away
it's hedge, and it will be destroyed …*" (Isaiah 5:5a). So too it is with His

---

[8] *Life Application Study Bible, NLT* (Wheaton, IL: Tyndale House Publishers, Inc.,
1996), 836.

children today. God will protect us as long as we stay faithful to Him: "*For the Lord God is our sun and our shield. He gives us grace and glory. The Lord will withhold no good thing from those who do what is right*" (Psalm 84:11, NLT).

Every day we get up, get dressed, and go about our lives. We go for a walk or get in our cars and run errands or drive to other provinces or states. We fly to other countries or gather together in groups and return home safely. But do we know how many times the Lord actually protects us from harm? We are truly blessed if the Lord has kept His hedge of protection around us. If we walk away from Him, He will remove His protection and we'll be on our own: "*Be my rock of safety, where I can always hide …*" (Psalm 71:3a, NLT). We have the assurance that we are always welcome to be under God's protection. Just be true to Him.

Day Thirty-Nine

NEVER ALONE

Joseph was in prison when Pharaoh's baker and cup-bearer (wine taster) joined him there. The two had separate dreams that Joseph interpreted. The baker dreamed that he would be killed, and he was. The cup-bearer's dream was that he would be released back into Pharaoh's court. "*Pharaoh's chief cup-bearer, however, forgot all about Joseph, never giving him another thought*" (Genesis 40:23, NLT). At that point I wonder if Joseph thought that God had forgotten him too. In God's timing, Joseph was released and became second in command to Pharaoh. The plan was to save the Israelites from starvation during the coming seven years of famine.

God spoke with Moses on Mount Sinai and told him to take the Israelites to the Promised Land. Moses said he couldn't do it alone and asked God to send someone with him. "*And the Lord replied, 'I myself will go with you and give you success.' For Moses had said, 'If you aren't going with us, don't let us move a step from this place'*" (Exodus 33:14–15, TLB). We are assured by God's words that He goes with us always, and as I've said before, God does not lie. "*The eyes of the Lord are on the righteous, and His ears are open to their cry*" (Psalm 34:15, NKJV).

We face many difficulties in life, and at times it seems like the Lord is deaf and doesn't hear us, but of course He does. He walks with us even when we feel alone. "… *I will never leave you nor forsake you*" (Hebrews 13:5b, NKJV).

God is always accessible, so we don't need to be in a specific location to talk to Him. All we need to do is call His name and He hears us. Unlike a cell phone that can lose reception, God is always there. In despair, in good times, He is always available, because His Spirit is in us. He's as close as He can be.

Day Forty
GUIDING WITH GOODNESS

*"Show me your ways, Lord, teach me Your paths. Guide
me in your truth and teach me, for you are God my
Savior, and my hope is in you all day long."*
(Psalm 25:4–5)

*"The Lord says, 'I will guide you along the best pathway
for your life. I will advise you and watch over you!'"*
(Psalm 32:8, NLT)

Whenever we traveled by car, I always got a map to follow. As I navigated, I followed it closely. I hated to be lost and waste time finding our way back, mainly because we were missing the things we really wanted to see. On bus tours the guide shows us and tells us about things we'd miss on our own. So too it is with the Lord as our guide. We have to decide if we want to go it on our own or let the Lord guide. If we study His map, the Bible, and obey what it says, He will guide us onto the right path.

"Oh, taste and see that the Lord is good; Blessed is the man who trusts in Him!" (Psalm 34:8, NKJV). I like to taste different kinds of food, especially when traveling. Different countries and cultures all have dishes that represent their nationalities. If we don't try new food, we could miss out on a new favorite dish. "*Taste and see*" means that God wants us to try Him, and as we inhale His aroma, and taste His goodness to us, we can trust that "... *all things work together for good to those who love God* ..." (Romans 8:28a, NKJV).

> *The Lord is merciful and compassionate, slow to get angry and filled with unfailing love. The Lord is good to everyone. He showers compassion on all His creation. All of Your works will thank you, Lord, and Your faithful followers will praise you.* (Psalm 145:8–10, NLT)

God loves us and has done so many good things for us, so we need to do our part and love Him, praise Him, and do good for others out of love. King David wrote many psalms in which he praised and thanked God for His goodness to him. God is blessed when we worship Him.

Day Forty-One

FRIENDS

"After David had finished talking with Saul, he met Jonathan, the king's son. There was an immediate bond between them, for Jonathan loved David."
(1 Samuel 18:1, NLT)

They were loyal, lifetime friends who went through hard times together but never betrayed each other.

Mary, Martha, and Lazarus of Bethany were close friends with Jesus. He frequently ate meals with them and would stay with them. Jesus loved them: "*This is the Mary who later poured the expensive perfume on the Lord's feet and wiped them with her hair*" (John 11:2a, NLT).

"*There are 'friends' who destroy each other, but a real friend sticks closer than a brother*" (Proverbs 18:24, NLT). I'm sure many of us have been betrayed by a friend; however, the ultimate betrayal was experienced by Jesus: "*Going at once to Jesus, Judas said, 'Greetings, Rabbi!' and kissed Him. Jesus replied, 'Do what you came for, friend'*" (Matthew 26:49–50a).

Friendships do change when we lose a loved one to death or divorce. Friends we used to have now avoid us, almost to the point that we feel like the lepers in the Old Testament that passed by and called out, "*Unclean! Unclean!*" (Leviticus 13:45, NLT). They don't want to be near us.

Day Forty-Two
FRIENDS (PART TWO)

I belong to a ladies' Bible study group that has been together for thirty-plus years. We're made up of country women, mostly farmers' wives, now retired to the city. At our Christmas wind-up a few years ago, I wrote about our long time together:

"During the thirty-plus years of our Bible study, there have been many changes. We have seen our kids grow up, graduate, go to college or Bible school, find jobs, fall in love, marry, and have children of their own. We have seen death, divorce, cancer, heart problems, other health issues, and surgeries. There have been wanted and unwanted changes of address. We have laughed together, cried together, played together, eaten together, prayed together, and some have traveled together. We have had discussions on hunting, fishing, gardening, canning, baking, cooking, and of course children and grandchildren. We prayed together about needs we had, and as farming goes, we prayed about seeding and harvest."

"We don't always agree, but it has never divided us. We as a group have strived to be obedient to the Lord, to be wise, and to be women of God. We desire to be good examples to others and to trust the Lord and each other. We praise and thank the Lord for what He has done for each of us. He truly deserves all the praise and thanks given to Him. We have seen some ladies in our group pass away or leave us, but there always seems to be someone else to join us. God does provide. We have a love for each other that can only come from the Lord. We have been faithful in our service to Him and for Him, and He has blessed us. We have shared each other's burdens and griefs. We have comforted each other in times of loneliness, sickness, and heartache. We still do service for our churches and our community. I know that pleases the Lord. God has always protected us, even in times we weren't aware of. He has been there. He answers when we call and loves to spend time with us as we study His Word and pray together.

"As I look around our group, I see that we are aging. We have aches and pains in areas of our bodies that we didn't even know we had. Lovingly, we still pray for each other and we love to meet together. As seniors, our desires have changed, our health has changed, our families and addresses have changed, but our love for the Lord has not. I know we have all grown in the Lord these past thirty-plus years. What a blessing!" (I might add that there are twelve ladies in the group.)

Being friends with God will last a lifetime if we honor and obey Him. He keeps His promises to us, tells the truth, listens to our every word, and guides us to the right path. He is loyal and stays with us when others walk away. He is our strength. He is our encourager. He picks us up when we fall down and comforts us in times of sorrow. He cries with us when we are in pain, and I believe He smiles when we please Him.

Day Forty-Three

GIFTS, TALENTS, AND ABILITIES

As I struggled to put this section together, I came to realize that all three words in the title are intertwined. On the spiritual side, we know that Jesus is a gift from God given to us for our salvation. We know that when Jesus went back to heaven, He sent us the gift of the Holy Spirit. On the personal level, God has gifted us, His creation, with many gifts.

Jesus is the gift that excels all gifts: "… *the free gift of God is eternal life through Christ Jesus our Lord*" (Romans 6:23b, NLT); "… *Repent and be baptized … in the name of Jesus Christ for the forgiveness of your sins. And you will receive the gift of the Holy Spirit*" (Acts 2:38). The God-given gifts of Jesus and the Holy Spirit are the core of Christianity. It's God's nature to show us His love through His Son's life, death, and resurrection.

In Romans 12 and 1 Corinthians 12, Paul tells believers that God has given the spiritual gifts that will strengthen the churches. These gifts are still relevant in our churches today.

God has given each of us the ability to do certain things well. So if God has given you the ability to prophesy, then prophesy whenever you can—as often as your faith is strong enough to receive a message from God. If your gift is that of serving others, serve them well. If you are a teacher, do a good job teaching. If you are a preacher, see to it that your sermons are strong and helpful. If God has given you money, be generous in helping others with it. If God has given you administrative ability and put you in charge of the work of others, take the responsibility seriously. Those who offer comfort to the sorrowing should do so with Christian cheer. (Romans 12:6–8, TLB)

There are different kinds of gifts, but the same Spirit ... To one there is given through the Spirit a message of wisdom, to another a message of knowledge ... to another faith ... to another gifts of healing ... to another miraculous power ... to another distinguishing between spirits [discernment] ... to another speaking in different kinds of tongues [languages] ... All these are the work of one and the same Spirit, and He gives them to each one, just as He determines. (1 Corinthians 12:4, 8–11).

Day Forty-Four

GIFTS, TALENTS, AND ABILITIES (PART TWO)

*God has given each of you a gift from his great variety
of spiritual gifts. Use them well to serve one another. Do
you have the gift of speaking? Then speak as though God
himself were speaking through you. Do you have the gift
of helping others? Do it with all the strength and energy
that God supplies. Then everything you do will bring
glory to God through Jesus Christ …*
(1 Peter 4:10–11, NLT)

King David was a skilled musician, singer, and writer of numerous
songs found in the Psalms. He played the harp for King Saul
whenever a "*tormenting spirit*" came upon him, and the spirit would go
away (1 Samuel 16:23, NLT). In Amos 6:5, King David was called a
great musician. I don't imagine he took any music lessons!

While researching I read that some who are truly gifted are born
with their talents and abilities. An example of this is a pianist by the
name of Anthony Berger. When he was five years old, he came home
from church, sat down at the piano, and without a note in front of him
he beautifully played the hymn he'd heard at church. He went on to be
an accomplished gospel and secular pianist.

A talent or ability may be natural or may need training and practice.
Years ago, my husband and I traveled numerous times with our friends,

Allan and Sheila. Allan and I were both playing for a southern gospel group, so inevitability we would re-kindle our ongoing debate about natural gifts and developed talents and abilities in the area of music. Most debates ended with Sheila asking us to end our discussion. Recently, we've agreed that some people are gifted in unexplainable ways, and some talents do need developing. The difference can be seen in his and my talent. He shared with me that he never took a guitar lesson but was inspired by a friend who was an excellent guitar player, and that gave him the desire to play. Today, he too is an excellent guitar player. I always needed notes to play the keyboard. I did improve by playing with practice, but I had to work at my talent and never became a Mozart. So really, the debate is settled. Some have natural inborn talents, and some need to develop their talents; however, they are all God-given.

Day Forty-Five

GIFTS, TALENTS, AND ABILITIES (PART THREE)

My ladies' Bible study group conducted a little exercise that named some of the gifts, talents, and abilities we saw in each other. Some of our gifts are mentioned in the scriptures; others pertain to what God has given to us on a personal level. We found that whatever the talent or ability given to us, some were gifted in certain areas, and others had absolutely no desire to pursue any of the abilities others possess. That makes each one of us unique in God's sight.

Some are excellent cooks and bakers. Some create beautiful crafts, which includes ornamental freehand painting. Some are talented interior decorators, and we have a carpenter. Out of doors there are some that have a "green thumb" and design beautiful yards and successful vegetable gardens … others, not so much!

We have encouragers; some have the gift of faith, and others can easily forgive. We have intercessory prayers, and others have the gift of discernment. We as friends are trustworthy and loyal. We see obedience to the Lord and thankfulness for God's goodness as well as humility and the desire to serve others who are in need by doing volunteer work in the church and community. There is compassion, patience, and unconditional love for others. Lastly, some are blessed with the gift of hospitality: *"Don't forget to show hospitality to strangers, for some who have done this have entertained angels without realizing it!"* (Hebrews 13:2, NLT).

"... Christ has given each of us special abilities—whatever He wants us to have out of his rich storehouse of gifts ... when Christ returned triumphantly to heaven after his resurrection ... he gave generous gifts to men" (Ephesians 4:7, 8b, TLB). We develop many personality traits as we go through life, but if we're steadfast and genuine in pursuing our Lord, He will develop whatever gifts, talents, and abilities we need to live in the power of His love.

Day Forty-Six

INJUSTICE

"The Lord gives righteousness and justice to all
who are treated unfairly."
(Psalm 103:6, NLT)

How many times have we said of a situation, "That's not fair." I know I have. When troubles come up against us or we're sinned against and don't see justice on our behalf, we wonder why. But God is fair, and all will be judged according to the injustice:

God Himself is the standard of justice. He uses His power according to His own moral perfection. Thus, whatever He does is fair, even if we don't understand it. Our response is to appeal directly to Him."[9]

I watched a news story about a gunman who had gone into a Baptist church in Texas and killed twenty-six people and wounded numerous others. Twelve of the dead were children, and we say, "Life isn't fair!" In Psalms 75:2, we read that God does do justice: "… *At the time I have planned, I will bring justice against the wicked*" (NLT).

---

[9] *Life Application Study Bible, NLT* (Wheaton, IL: Tyndale House Publishers, Inc., 1996), 813.

I [Solomom] also noticed that under the sun there is evil in the courtroom. Yes, even the courts of law are corrupt! I said to myself, "In due season God will judge everyone, both good and bad, for all their deeds." (Ecclesiastes 3:16–17, NLT)

I read an article about a man who was on trial for murdering a young girl. The justice system failed, and a mistrial was declared. The girl's parents wept, wondering where the justice was. We see in verse seventeen above that in God's timing, justice will come.

"Are we saying, then, that God was unfair? Of course not!" (Romans 9:14, NLT). God chose Jacob for the responsibility of fathering the twelve tribes of Israel. Esau would be ruler of a smaller nation, Edom. God loved them both but chose Jacob. God is sovereign and trustworthy and knew the best choice to lead Israel.

We question God when we believe He's being unfair or unjust, but the question is answered in Genesis 18:25b by Abraham: "... *Will not the Judge of all the earth do right?"* God's courtroom is fair and just. All things come before Him, and all things will be judged according to His will and grace.

Day Forty-Seven

LOVE EACH OTHER

Jesus said: "'*Love the Lord your God with all your heart and with all your soul and with all your mind and with all your strength.' The second is this: 'Love your neighbour as yourself.'*" (Mark 12:30–31a). These two verses capture the issue of love. We as Christians are called to love the Lord, and with His love within us, love and care for others.

On the television news I saw that an Australian news reporter had been freed from an Egyptian jail where he had been held for four hundred days. In an interview he stated that he was happy to be released but was very concerned for the friends he had to leave behind. I don't know if he was a Christian, but I know he loved and cared about the friends he'd made. Leaving his friends was difficult.

Jesus said, "*Your love for one another will prove to the world that you are my disciples*" (John 13:35, NLT). I read about an organization called "Love, INC." and discovered that this group's focus was on trying to get churches to help the needy world. "Love, INC." means "Love In the Name of Christ." Let's prove our love for the Lord by helping the needy that we see all around us.

"If you love those who love you, what credit is that to you? Even sinners love those who love them … But love your enemies, do good to them..." (Luke 6:32, 35a). A little six-year-old boy gave us a nugget of wisdom when he spoke about love: "If you want to love better, you should start with a friend that you hate." Children seem to grasp life's issues easier than adults. We are called by God to love both the "lovely and unlovely alike."

Today we hear people say, "Love you," almost as a greeting. We say it to our spouses, family, and friends. Rarely do we hear people say, "I love you" to the Lord. Has the meaning of love changed in this information age we live in? Has love become just a feeling, emotion, or expression? Without actions, love is just an empty word. Jesus proved His love for us with the action of the cross. We need to prove our love for Jesus by being obedient to and spending time with Him by talking and listening to Him. Then we need to put into practice His love through commitment, backed up by honor and respect for those in our lives. We need to show love, not just say it.

Day Forty-Eight

GOD-GIVEN WISDOM: NEW TESTAMENT

*"When the time came for the purification rites required
by the Law of Moses, Joseph and Mary took him [Jesus]
to Jerusalem to present Him to the Lord ... And the
child [Jesus] grew and became strong; he was filled with
wisdom, and the grace of God was on him."*
(Luke 2:22, 40)

*"Oh, how great are God's riches and wisdom and knowledge ...
For everything comes from him and exists by his power and is
intended for his glory. All glory to him forever! Amen."*
(Romans 11:33a, 36, NLT)

*"Who is wise and understanding among you? Let them show
it by their good life, by deeds done in the humility that comes
from wisdom. But if you harbor bitter envy and selfish ambition
in your hearts, do not boast about it or deny the truth. Such
'wisdom' does not come down from heaven but is earthly,
unspiritual, demonic ... But the wisdom that comes from heaven
is first of all pure; then peace-loving, considerate, submissive, full
of mercy and good fruit, impartial and sincere."*
(James 3:13–15, 17)

I believe these verses show the difference between foolishness and God-given wisdom. We can know if we are wise or foolish by what is said when we open our mouths and speak, or by the way we act. We can become wise, knowledgeable, and intellectual about what all the world has to offer, but by learning the way of the Lord and being obedient to His teachings from Scripture, and dwelling in His holiness, we can become truly wise.

> *If you want to know what God wants you to do, ask him, and he will gladly tell you, for he is always ready to give a bountiful supply of wisdom to all who ask him; he will not resent it.* (James 1:5, TLB)

I leave you with my prayer: "I ask for wisdom, Lord. I need to be wise in all my decisions. I ask for understanding in each opportunity that comes my way. Help me to remember that I am not alone and that You will guide me to Your wisdom, especially when the challenges are overwhelming. Help me to focus on what is in store for my life and forget past unwise decisions. Help me to move forward in Your power. Amen!"

Day Forty-Nine

THORNS IN THE SPIRIT

*Therefore I [Jesus] tell you, do not worry about your life,
what you will eat or drink; or about your body, what
you will wear ... Can any one of you by worrying add a
single hour to your life? ... But seek first His kingdom
and His righteousness, and all these things will be given
to you as well. Therefore do not worry about tomorrow,
for tomorrow will worry about itself. Each day
has enough trouble of its own.*
(Matthew 6:25, 27, 33–34)

Being honest here, I can say that I have worried and still worry from time to time. In the past I've worried to the point of mental, physical, and spiritual fatigue. At the age of sixty-three, I found myself alone and worried about my life. Would I find a place to live, and could I afford the rent? Could I find a part-time job? When I found a job in ladies' wear at a local department store, I worried that I didn't have nice enough clothes to work in. Later when I had to take classes to get a better job, I worried if I could pass the mandatory test I had to write, especially at my age. I worried about losing weight. Was I too broken to eat, or was I worried that the growths my doctor found were cancer? And after the surgeries, would the cancer come back again? These worries were all giants in my life, and only when I gave them all to "the giant slayer," my

Lord, could I eventually triumph over worry. I regained my trust in the Lord, because deep down I knew that God was in charge and in control. I had to do a complete heart adjustment and find the Lord's peace again.

Jesus said, *"Peace I leave with you; My peace I give you … Do not let your hearts be troubled and do not be afraid"* (John 14:27). God does give His peace when we search for it. We humans worry as we struggle with daily problems, and we wonder what life has in store for us, but as believers we are blessed to have a friend in Jesus, who will strengthen our faith so we can carry on and trust Him in all things.

In Matthew 13, Jesus tells the parable of the four soils, where worry is explained as the seed that fell on thorns and was choked out, making it unfruitful. So too it is with us. Worry will choke out every ounce of faith and trust that we have in the Lord. That's why it's so important to seek the Lord first, trust that He has everything under control, and give up all worry and anxiety. The Lord knows all our troubles, and as He promised, He will look after us.

Day Fifty

FAITH ABOUNDS

*"Faith shows the reality of what we hope for; it is the
evidence of things we cannot see."*
(Hebrews 11:1, NLT)

My favorite faith story in the Bible is about the woman who was sick for a long time.

*And suddenly, a woman who had a flow of blood for twelve years
came from behind and touched the hem of His garment. For she
said to herself, "If only I may touch His garment, I shall be made
well." But Jesus turned around, and when He saw her He said,
"Be of good cheer, daughter; your faith has made you well." And
the woman was made well from that hour.* (Matthew 9:20–22,
NKJV)

In Bible times, a woman with a "flow of blood" wasn't allowed to go out, as she was "unclean" by law. If caught, she would be stoned. This amazing woman knew that if she could just get to Jesus, just touch His garment, she would be healed. She believed Jesus could heal her when all other attempts had failed. Her overwhelming faith made her whole.

"*… Christ is all, and is in all*" (Colossians 3:11). In this chapter, Paul talks about new life in Christ that begins when we make a commitment to follow Him. In a different context, I'm going to show how we can have faith in the Lord ... always. I have flown numerous times in my life in all types of circumstances, so I'm going to use a weather-related example. At times I've been in heavy clouds and strong winds that caused turbulence and unrest in the airplane. Of course we were told to put our seat belts on and sit down. When pilots can't see the ground, they rely on instruments and computers to guide them. Fortunately, they are trained for such circumstances. Faith is like that. We're flying blind, but we can trust in our pilot, the Lord, to get us safely to the end of our flight. If *"Christ is all, and is in all,"* I have to have faith that He, our pilot, is in control. I can honestly say that there have been times when my faith needed a "seat belt," and I prayed for a safe flight and landing ... in life and in the airplane.

"The faithful love of the Lord never ends! His mercies never cease. Great is His faithfulness; his mercies begin afresh each morning" (Lamentations 3:22–23, NLT). There are times when our faith is weak, but God remains faithful and will help us as He promised.

Day Fifty-One
SHIPWRECKED VERSUS RESCUED

"… those who hope in me will not be disappointed."
(Isaiah 49:23b)

We have great expectations for our lives. We want a great marriage, family, job, friends, and good health. With expectation comes disappointment. We feel abandoned, hurt, and angry, and we question God as to why we go through trials. Where is the justice? What purpose is there for us to even live? Why were we even born? When depression sets in, we need to dwell in the hope the Lord instils deep in our spirits and on the words in Psalm 42:11: "*Why am I discouraged? Why is my heart so sad? I will put my hope in God! I will praise him again—my Savior and my God!*" (NLT). Rescue comes when we turn our disappointments over to the Lord and praise Him in spite of our circumstances. He will lift us up! When we have been rescued, we need to re-focus and turn our sadness to joy and become encouragers ourselves.

In Acts 4:36–37, we learn about Barnabas. He was such a wonderful encourager that he was called "Son of Encouragement" by the apostles. His gift was to encourage. There's always someone who needs to be encouraged, and it's an effective way to draw people to the gospel of Jesus. "*If your gift is to encourage others, be encouraging …*" (Romans 12:8a, NLT).

Every letter that Paul wrote to the early churches was filled with encouraging words: "*The people read it* [Paul's letter] *and were glad for its encouraging message*" (Acts :15:31); "*So encourage each other to build each other up, just as you are already doing*" (1 Thessalonians 5:11, TLB); "*So let's not get tired of doing what is good. At just the right time we will reap a harvest of blessing if we don't give up*" (Galatians 6:9, NLT); "*But encourage one another daily, as long as it is called 'Today' …*" (Hebrews 3:13a). Today, let's start encouraging others. It could be a phone call or text, or saying a kind word to someone, or praying for a friend who is sick. Maybe our kindness will save a life or help someone's unbelief. Look for ways to lift someone's spirit. There are always people who need encouraging.

There are discouragers and encouragers in the Bible. Job's three friends are the best example of discouragers. They could have left Job feeling hopeless. In the New Testament, Paul and Barnabas were great examples of being encouragers. Today we have the choice to be negative and destroy someone's spirit, or to look to the Lord for guidance and be someone who lifts the spirits of the broken-hearted. Do we want to be shipwrecked and drifting, or rescued and safe in the arms of Jesus?

Day Fifty-Two

It's Your Fault

Blaming God started way back in the Garden of Eden:

> *… The man [Adam] said, "The woman you put here with me—she gave me some fruit from the tree and I ate it." Then the Lord God said to the woman, "What is this you have done?" The woman said, "The serpent deceived me, and I ate."* (Genesis 3:12–13)

Blame somebody!

When the people of Nineveh repented, Jonah had a pity party, so he complained to the Lord about it: *"Didn't I say … that you would do this, Lord?"* (Jonah 4:2, NLT) *"… Just kill me now, Lord"* (Jonah 4:3, NLT) … *"The Lord replied, 'Is it right for you to be angry about this?'"* (Jonah 4:4, NLT). Job blamed God when he said *"But it is God who has wronged me, capturing me in his net"* (Job 19:6, NLT). Job blamed God when in fact it was Satan who caused it all. We need to be careful who we blame when things go wrong.

"And don't murmur against God and His dealings with you …" (1 Corinthians 10:10a, TLB). Paul is speaking to the Israelites here, but

it absolutely applies to us. When I started to write this book and read my journals, I realized that I blamed God for allowing my life to go the way it did. The things I wrote against Him broke my heart, and I had to ask the Lord, my Creator, to forgive me. Thankfully He has very broad shoulders! Bishop Dale C. Bronner, on his television program *Power for Living*, once said that when a situation arose that was troubling him, he "got in God's face instead of being at His feet."

"*... he is God, the one who rules over everything and is worthy of eternal praise! Amen.* [Or may God, who rules over everything, be praised forever, Amen]." (Romans 9:5b, NLT). How many of us really understand the power of God? We are so stuck in the problems in our lives that we fail to grasp a single speck of His absolute life-giving and creative power. He keeps the earth turning, the sun, moon, stars, and oceans in their place. He has the power to snuff out or sustain life in a second, and sometimes we still point a finger at Him and blame Him for whatever is going on in our lives. God doesn't need us to be His prosecuting attorney, and we have no authority to cross-examine Him. He still is God—even when we are in pain.

"*The Lord is good. When trouble comes, he is the place to go! And he knows everyone who trusts in him!*" (Nahum 1:7, TLB). God is good and He wants us to remember that life happens, but He is still God. We have to believe in His goodness. He is patient with us and doesn't judge us for trying to understand why certain things happen. As we turn to Him, He will faithfully pour out "*the riches of his glory*" upon us (Romans 9:23, NLT).

Day Fifty-Three
THE THRONE OF SELF

"This is what the Lord says: 'Heaven is my throne,
and the earth is my footstool.'"
(Isaiah 66:1a)

We keep God on His throne by honoring Him in prayer and worshipfully praising Him with a thankful heart. When we put our trust in Him and are obedient, He will keep His rightful place on His throne of grace. *"I will praise you as long as I live, lifting up my hands to you in prayer"* (Psalm 63:4, NLT); *"Let us come before Him with thanksgiving and extol Him with music and song"* (Psalm 95:2); *"Exalt the Lord our God and worship at his footstool; he is holy"* (Psalm 99:5). Take some time to study the Psalms. They are full of verses of praise to the Lord.

When things are going well, we don't rely on the Lord as much. He slowly slips off His throne, and we replace Him with ourselves. We're pleased with our lives and become self-sufficient, proud, and arrogant. The Bible contains stories of men who become too proud and self-sufficient. King Saul in 1 Samuel 15:13 thought he could take the place of the priest and make his own sacrifice to God. In Genesis 11:4–8, the people were so proud of themselves, they tried to build a tower (Babel) to reach heaven. The Lord disciplined them by giving them different languages, so they couldn't understand each other. Even the disciples thought very highly of themselves: *"Now there was also a dispute among them, as to which of them should be considered the greatest"* (Luke 22:24, NKJV). Jesus said: *"Students are not greater than their teacher, and slaves are not greater than their master"* (Matthew 10:24, NLT). At this point, I found a little blurb in my notes that said "Leonardo de Vinci's paint brush was not greater than the artist himself." So true!

I've talked with and listened to numerous people over the years who struggled with low self-esteem and felt worthless because they were told that they were, and they believed it. We're told that we are not attractive and our appearance needs help. Our personality, intelligence, abilities, and capabilities are criticized. Some people are verbally attacked, and some are physically abused, or their character, belief system, and faith are questioned. Recently I heard of a woman who was rejected by her husband because she had health problems, which led him to infidelity. Many people are cheated on and their marriages and homes broken apart. The workplace is riddled with sexual, verbal, and emotional misconduct. Families destroy each other with hurtful words and actions. As a result of this brokenness, people feel discouraged, unloved, alone, and afraid. Low self-esteem turns into self-pity, and lives are destroyed.

Day Fifty-Four
THE THRONE OF SELF (PART TWO)

People from every corner of the world today are mentally, physically, emotionally, and sexually abused. They are over-wrought with despair and give up. Some become destructive and turn to drugs and alcohol. The Bible tells us that Jesus is the answer. "… *Come to me, all of you who are weary and carry heavy burdens, and I will give you rest*" (Matthew 11:28, NLT). The answer to our pain is to surrender our whole self to the Lord, grab on to His nail-pierced hands, and He will make us new.

"*Then God said, 'Let us make people [man]human beings in our image, to be like us*'" (Genesis 1:26a, NLT). Our self-worth should come from being made to be like God, not because of how we look or what we say or do. When we're told that we are imperfect, no good, or whatever negative words are spoken against us, God Himself is being criticized, because He made us—and He doesn't make junk.

God wants us to look in the mirror and see a person of worth. God says to us, "You are beautiful because I created you, and you are perfect in my sight. Each one of us is unique—there is no one exactly like us. Even twins have different personalities. Once we realize how precious we are to the Lord and ask to be restored as a "woman of worth," He will take His rightful place back on the throne and make us new again. *"He who was seated on the throne said, 'I am making everything new!'"* (Revelation 21:5a). Evangelist Joyce Meyer, on her television program *Joyce Meyer Enjoying Everyday* Life, once said: "Don't run away from hard things, because God will turn you into something magnificent."

> *What joy for those whose strength comes from the Lord ... When they walk through the Valley of Weeping, it will become a place of refreshing springs ... They will continue to grow stronger ... O Lord God of Heaven's Armies hear my prayer ... For the Lord God is our sun and shield. He gives grace and glory. The Lord will withhold no good thing from those who do what is right. O Lord of Heaven's Armies, what joy for those who trust in you.* (Psalm 84:5–12, NLT)

Being able to leave self at the "footstool" of God's throne is a journey. When we spend time with Him, we can achieve unimaginable peace and joy in our spirits and, best of all, be restored! A brand new you!

Day Fifty-Five

NEW NAME—NEW YOU

*"Therefore, if anyone is in Christ, the new creation has
come: The old has gone, the new is here!"*
(2 Corinthians 5:17)

When we ask the Lord to forgive our sins and we give our hearts
to Him, He begins to recreate us. We are given the new name
of Christian, or Christ follower. In 2007, I got an e-mail from a friend,
Sandy, that shows the change in us after we give our hearts to the Lord:

> A woman was asked by a co-worker, "What is it like to be a
> Christian?" The co-worker replied, "It's like being a pumpkin.
> God picks you up from the patch, brings you in, and washes
> all the dirt off of you. Then He cuts off the top and scoops out
> all the 'yucky' stuff. He removes the seeds of doubt, hate, and
> greed. Then He carves a new smiley face and puts a light inside
> you to shine for all the world to see!"

In the Bible, some people were given new names and some were
changed by God Himself. Biblical names also had special meanings. In
Genesis 17:5, God changes Abram's name to Abraham. Abram means
"exalted father;" Abraham means "father of many." In Genesis 17:15–16,
God changes Sarai's name to Sarah, which means "mother of a nation."

In Genesis 32:28, Jacob's name is changed by God to "Israel," which means "God struggles" or "one who struggles with God." In the New Testament, Saul's name was changed to the apostle Paul. In Revelation 2:17, God tells us that when we get to heaven, we will be given new names known only to the one who receives it and God Himself. God knows my name here on earth. When I pray, I don't have to introduce myself to Him and say, "Darlene, here!" When we worship at the feet of Jesus, He knows who we are—there is no guessing involved.

A side note here: When I was researching names in the Bible, I realized that not one person is called by their last name. A few examples of many are Joshua, son of Nun. King David, son of Jesse, and Isaiah, son of Amos. Some are identified by tribe, such as Judah or Benjamin. God knows their last names as He knows ours. We are not nameless to Him. When we ask the Lord into our lives, a new life begins. We are given a complete "spiritual makeover." Change takes time, but God is our Author, and in Him is new life.

Day Fifty-Six

IS THAT YOU, LORD?

Jesus says: "*Here I am! I stand at the door and knock. If anyone hears my voice and opens the door, I will come in …*" (Revelation 3:20). If God wants to come into our hearts and forgive our sins, we need to listen to His voice, open the door, and let Him in, because He is the only way to heaven.

I read the story of two shepherds who were walking their sheep down a road. One group was going east; the other, west. As they came together, the shepherds stopped to talk to each other for a while. The sheep mingled together, and at a glance they couldn't tell which sheep belonged to which shepherd. When it was time to continue their journey, the shepherds spoke and the sheep followed the voice of their shepherd. They separated and continued on the way they were going. In John 10:1–5, Jesus tells the parable of the sheepfold. The shepherd calls and the sheep follow His voice. Jesus is our Shepherd, and we need to recognize His voice and follow Him.

"*Then I* [Isaiah] *heard the Lord asking, 'Whom shall I send as a messenger to my people? Who will go?' And I said, 'Lord, I'll go! Send me*" (Isaiah 6:8, TLB). This verse seems to be written just for me at this time in my life, and it relates to this book that I'm working on. It has taken me many months to write, and I get discouraged when I hear of people who write two or more books a year. I wonder why God wants me to write. I honestly think my friends are getting sick of hearing "I'm writing" when they ask me what I'm doing. The clear message I have from the Lord to write gives way to pleading with Him to let me put all my notes away, lock them in a drawer, and throw away the key. Then my stomach meets my throat, and my heart does a flip, and I know I have to finish it. God is not a quitter, and if I follow God's voice—neither am I.

When we ask the question, "Is that You, Lord?" we can be assured that the answer is His if what is said lines up with Scripture and is within God's character. He won't tell us anything that's not part of Him, so we need to ask if what we hear will help us grow spiritually and restore our souls and give us peace when we do what He asks. "*Call to Me, and I will answer you …*" (Jeremiah 33:3a, NKJV). With today's busyness, there are many voices in our heads pulling us in different directions, but when we are quiet before the Lord, the Holy Spirit will help us recognize the voice of the Lord above all others.

Day Fifty-Seven

WHO'S IN YOUR CLOUD?

In this information age, there's a resource on computers, iPhones, iPads, and other devices, called "The Cloud." I, however, come from an age where clouds are in the sky. In the Bible, clouds are always connected or linked with God. The Old Testament prophets speak of God in the clouds, and that continues right to the end of the Bible when Jesus returns from heaven to gather His saints. In Genesis 9:13, clouds hold the promised rainbow. In Exodus 13:21–22, God is in the cloud by day and in the pillar of fire by night. In Exodus 16:10b, God is the guiding cloud. In Exodus 19:9, God is a thick, or dense, cloud. In Exodus 24:15a, God is in the cloud that covers Mound Sinai where the Ten Commandments are given. In Leviticus 16:1–2, God is in the cloud that covers the mercy seat (the ark of the covenant). In Numbers 9:15–23, God is in the cloud that covers the tent of meeting (tabernacle). In 2 Chronicles 5:13–14, after the temple Solomon built is completed, God enters the most holy place (the Holy of Holies), and His cloud fills the temple. In Psalm 68:4b, God rides upon the clouds, and in Psalm 104:3b, the clouds are His chariot. In Psalm 147:8a, God covers the heavens with clouds, and in Ecclesiastes 11:3a, when the clouds get too heavy, the rain pours down. In Isaiah 19:1b, God rides on a swift cloud, and my favorite—Nahum 1:3c: "*The billowing clouds are the dust beneath His feet*" (NLT).

In the New Testament, Jesus takes Peter, James, and John with Him to the Mount of Transfiguration, and a cloud covers them. They are terrified. God the Father speaks to them from the cloud (Luke 9:32–35). Jesus ascends back to heaven in a cloud in Acts 1:9, and in Revelation 1:7a we read: "*Behold, He is coming with the clouds, and every eye will see Him* …" (NASB).

I'm fascinated with clouds and what they represent in the Bible and in the sky. I watch The Weather Network on television to see what the clouds are doing and to learn what each type of cloud produces in the atmosphere. Clouds are given names according to their height and shape. Wind clouds and rain clouds look pretty normal, grey, and dismal. Thunder clouds that have hail in them look like an anvil. Hurricane clouds have a calm eye in the center of the circular movement of the clouds. Just as frightening are the "super cell" clouds that wrap themselves up in a cone shape and become tornadoes. My favorite clouds are called cumulonimbus. They look like giant marshmallows all gathered together, and they can produce rain.

Day Fifty-Eight

WHO'S IN YOUR CLOUD? (PART TWO)

Hebrews 11 is known as the faith chapter, and in Hebrews 12:1, the *"great cloud of witnesses"* are the people mentioned in the previous chapter. They too struggled with life problems, but they remained faithful to the Lord in their walk with Him.

Sometimes the Lord sends clouds into our lives such as sorrow, sickness, or heartache to draw us closer to Him. When we release our tears like raindrops from a storm cloud, the Lord refills the clouds with the "sunshine" of His love.

Sometimes we fill the clouds with idols instead of with God: "*Whenever you have thrown away your idols, I* [God] *have shown you my power*" (Isaiah 43:12a, TLB). In the Old Testament, Aaron forged a golden calf to worship (Exodus 32:1–8). Today our idols can be numerous things that take God out of the cloud. He is replaced by the worship of movie stars, athletes, and even our families, personal achievements, or possessions. We all know about *American Idol*. When whatever, or whoever, that is in our cloud becomes more important than the Lord, we become self-absorbed and detached from Him. All His power is blown away in the wind. If we're obsessed with the Lord, nothing will be in the cloud but Him. *"For in Him we live and move and exist ..."* (Acts 17:28a, NLT). Nothing should be more important than God. I've heard it said that we need to put God first, God second, and God third. When that happens, there's no room in our cloud for anybody or anything but Him.

I read a little notation that illustrates the cloud perfectly. Answer these questions: Would you invite special and important company over for a feast of microwaved leftovers? Would that make them feel special and important to you? The Lord doesn't want our leftovers either. He doesn't want to be second, third, or worse. He wants all of us. He wants our best, and He wants our hearts.

"You have covered yourself with a cloud so that no prayer can get through" (Lamentations 3:44). Isn't that the way it is with us sometimes? We pray and pray about something, but there seems to be no answer, so we say, "Are you there, Lord?" Or we wonder, "Where is God?" When we realize that He is there, gently telling us to get the idols out of our cloud and put Him back in, His power will be released and we'll see how awesome and majestic He is, and that He loves us and cares about us.

Day Fifty-Nine
WHERE IS GOD?

I heard a story about two little boys that were always in trouble and always in the middle of something gone wrong. The mother looking for help consulted a local pastor who had success in helping troubled children. The pastor spoke with the boys individually. The younger boy went first. With a loud, booming voice the pastor said to him, "Son do you know where God is?" The boy was too frightened to say anything. The pastor asked him again and shook his finger at the boy and yelled, "Where is God?" The boy screamed; bolted out the door; ran home and dove into the closet and shut the door. When the older brother found his younger brother in the closet he frantically asked, "What happened?" The boy in the closet breathlessly replied, "We're in big trouble this time; God is missing and they think we took Him." That's a cute little story, and sometimes it does feel like God is missing, but in reality, He never leaves us and we don't have to be afraid. He is in the closet with us.

Numerous Old Testament prophets and kings cried out to God when they felt abandoned by Him, and Jesus on the cross felt the same. King David said: "*My God, my God, why have you abandoned me?*" (Psalm 22:1, NLT). King David was often in distress and always cried out to

God; however, his psalms ended with praise to God for His goodness. In Matthew 27:46b, Jesus too cried out, *"My God, my God, why have you abandoned me?"* (NLT). But his Father was there. I believe that God darkened the sun and shook the earth because it was so heart-breaking for Him to watch His Son die in agony for a world that didn't care about Him or believe in Him (just a thought).

We often wonder where God is when we're alone and in physical and emotional pain, or when our marriages and families are torn apart. Where's God when we lose our jobs or homes? Or when we lose loved ones to tragedy or disease? What about when there's emotional, physical, and sexual abuse? It might not look like it, but the Lord is right there with His arms outstretched, because He loves us unconditionally—even if we point a finger at Him.

Jesus tells us that when we feel abandoned, we need to *"go into your* [our] *inner room, close your* [our] *door and pray to your* [our] *Father ..."* (Matthew 6:6a, NASB). When we have a close, personal relationship with the Lord through talking with Him, we don't have to ask, "Where are you, Lord?" He's right here, right now, wrapping His loving arms around us, holding us close. When we emotionally can't walk anymore, He will carry us. We are so blessed to have such a loving God.

Day Sixty

KNOWING GOD INTIMATELY

Paul says, "*I want to know Christ …*" (Philippians 3:10a). To know someone intimately, we need to make them our top priority and develop a deep, passionate love for them. So too it should be with the Lord. The deeper our walk with Him, the more of His characteristics are displayed in us, and the closer we are to Him.

To be like the Lord and to really get to know Him, there are things we need to do. We need to meditate on His Word and ask Him to show us what the words mean. He certainly speaks to us through Scripture. We also need to spend time with Him in prayer with praise, worship, and thankfulness. It's no different than in human relationships. We need to spend time together to know and understand each other. There must be complete trust in intimacy. If we don't trust the Lord, how can we be close? We need to make the Lord number one, not just in words but in actions.

Accepting the Lord as our Savior is only the first step to knowing Him. We need to give Him everything in our lives—our rights, our habits, and our doubts. Becoming intimate is a process. Just as in personal relationships, we need to work at it. Until we really see who the

Lord is, feel His presence, touch the hem of His garment, and develop a desire to be with Him, we never really enter into the close relationship we long for. When we get to the place in our spiritual walk where we can honestly say "… *Christ is all, and in all*" (Colossians 3:11b, NASB), then we know Him intimately.

I was paging through the television channel's programming and saw a title of a movie that intrigued me: *He's Just Not That into You*. I didn't check it out, so I don't know what it's about, but I can honestly say that the Lord would never say to us, "I'm just not that into you." The Holy Spirit is totally into us!

An old wives' tale says that when couples are together for many decades, they start to look like each other and can finish each other's sentences. So it should be with God. The more time we spend with Him, the more we'll look like Him and sound like Him. We need to be open and honest with God and hold nothing back from Him. When we totally surrender ourselves to Him, we can become as close to Him as the members of the Trinity are with each other. Do we want to be with the Lord more than with anybody else?

Day Sixty-One
HELD IN THE GRIP OF GOD'S LOVE

In Hebrews 6:18a and 19a, Paul gives us the answer for surviving a storm: "*He* [God] *has given us both His promise and His oath, two things we can completely count on, for it is impossible for God to tell a lie … This certain hope of being saved is a strong and trustworthy anchor for our souls …*" (TLB). A ship's anchor holds a boat steady. With God as our anchor, we are secured and can survive a storm. Sometimes we go through storms because God wants to teach us something either about ourselves or a troublesome situation. Maybe we don't want to give up something, such as a bad habit or someone who's not good for us. Storms are designed specifically for each individual, because the things we need to learn are for us only. Thankfully God never says, "You're on your own."

I love this little story from C.P. Hia about a plane ride that got really bumpy because they were going through a storm. The plane heaved and rolled like waves on the ocean. Passengers were trying to deal with the turbulence as best they could; of course, they were anxious. A little girl calmly sat in her seat reading a book, and when asked why she was so calm, she said, "My daddy is the pilot, and he's taking me home." The Lord is our pilot, and He's flying our plane.

In Mark 4:35–41, the disciples are caught in a storm, and their boat is taking on water. Jesus is in the back of the boat, asleep. The disciples wake Him up: "*Jesus stood up and commanded the wind, 'Be quiet!' and he said to the waves, 'Be still!' The wind died down, and there was a great calm*" (Mark 4:39, GNT). The disciples were with Jesus, yet they were terrified of the storm. When we have Jesus in our boat, or in the cockpit, we need not worry or panic. God is in control.

When God is our pilot and anchor and we're buckled in, or anchored in the grip of God's love, we will survive every storm.

Day Sixty-Two

SELAH, BE STILL AND KNOW

Throughout the Psalms we see the word, "Selah." It's a Hebrew musical word that means pause, and calmly think of that, and be lifted up. King David said: "*With my voice I was crying to the Lord, and He answered me from his holy mountain. Selah*" (Psalm 3:4, AMP). Some Bible translations use the word "Interlude" for Selah.

I read various Bible translations to understand the full meaning of a word or verse. Psalm 37 uses different ways of saying the same thing about being still before the Lord. In verse 1, the NLT tells us not to worry or envy. In verse 3, the AMP says to "*Trust [rely on and have confidence] in the Lord ...*" In verse 4, the NIV says, "*Take delight in the Lord, and he will give you the desires of your heart.*" If to delight means to give great pleasure or joy to, that means we are to do things that please and give joy to the Lord, while we wait. In verse 5, the NLT says to commit everything to Him and trust Him. In verse 7, the NKJV says "*Rest in the Lord, and wait patiently for Him ...*" In the dictionary, "rest" means to be still and take rest. That's like having a hectic, stressful day at work and then getting home, plopping ourselves down on the couch, putting our feet up, taking a deep breath, relaxing, and letting our bodies catch up with our souls. The NLT says, "*Be still in the presence of the Lord, and wait patiently …*"

I heard about a man and wife that often went fishing together. A friend asked them what they talked about all day, to which he replied, "We don't talk; we just fish." It really isn't the talking that makes a day enjoyable; it's quietly being with the one you love. If we rest in and spend time with the Lord, He will act on our behalf; however, we undoubtedly use a different clock than does God.

"*Stand silent! Know that I am God!*" (Psalm 46:10a, TLB). The NLT says "*Be silent.*" This verse reminds me of when I watched a police drama on television in which the police were told to "stand down" in a tense situation. The police lowered their guns and waited for their next orders. Sometimes we need to stand down, Selah (pause and calmly think) about what the Lord has planned for us, and just wait in His presence.

In this age of instant everything, "wait" is a foreign word. It's important to spend time in God's Word and in prayer. In our waiting, we need to praise the Lord, dwell in His goodness and beauty, be still, and wait. He will reply. As we wait in His presence, our question to Him should be: "What can I offer You?" Lovingly, He will honor us with the answer.

Day Sixty-Three

WHAT CAN I OFFER HIM?

What can I offer the Lord for all He has done for me? ...
I will ... praise the Lord's name for saving me ...
I will keep my promises to the Lord ... O Lord, I
am Your servant ... I will offer you a sacrifice of
thanksgiving and call on the name of the Lord.
(Psalm 116:12–14, 16–17, NLT)

We are to let the Holy Spirit fill and control us, and to sing and make music to the Lord. Paul tells us to give thanks to God for everything and submit to each other out of reverence for Christ (Ephesians 5:18b–21).

The Old Testament sacrifices were extremely more difficult to make than offerings are today. For each offering, a different sacrifice was required. Some required the sacrifice of certain animals and birds, grain, unleavened bread, and wine, to name a few. When Jesus gave His life as broken bread and poured-out wine, the sacrifices we give changed: "*Through Him, therefore, let us at all times offer up to God a sacrifice of praise* ..." (Hebrews 13:15a, AMP).

Praise is an act of worship. When we are filled with the Holy Spirit, we can praise the Lord wherever we are. We can praise Him with or without music. Praise is an attitude of the heart. The Lord wants us to keep our promises to Him and others, as broken promises can hurt. The

Lord also wants us to serve Him with our gifts. Jesus came to serve, so we should serve Him and others. Throughout the Bible we're told to be thankful. God wants us to give Him all that we are and all that we have, including our time, our possessions, and our lives. And we are to be thankful.

A singer on a Christmas special told the story behind the song "The Little Drummer Boy." The little boy wanted to give a gift to Jesus, but he had nothing to give Him. All he had was the gift of being a "drummer" that the Lord had given him. So he gave the gift back to Jesus by "drumming" for Him. He gave all he had to Jesus, and Jesus gave us all He had.

Paul says: "*For I am already being poured out like a drink offering, and the time for my departure is near*" (2 Timothy 4:6). In the Old Testament, a drink offering of wine was poured on the altar of sacrifice to God. This was a pleasing sacrifice to God. Paul poured out his life, because he wanted to please God. Jesus' blood on the cross was His drink offering to His Father, and His body was broken bread. What can we offer Him? EVERYTHING!

Day Sixty-Four

BROKEN BREAD AND POURED-OUT WINE

In the Old Testament tent of meeting was a room called the holy place. Everything in that room was a symbol of the coming Messiah and a foreshadowing of Jesus' life and death. In Exodus 25:23–31, God tells Moses to make a table of acacia wood and cover it with gold and put pitchers on it for the pouring out of drink offerings. He's to put the Bread of the Presence on the table and then make a lampstand of pure gold. In Leviticus, God instructs Moses to use fine flour and bake twelve loaves of bread and place them on the table in two rows of six. Pure frankincense is to be sprinkled on the bread as a memorial. For the lamp, he's to use pure olive oil (24:5–9). In Numbers 4:7–9, God shows the order of the cloths that were used to cover the table. They were to use blue cloth, then a scarlet cloth, and lastly sheepskins. The olive oil represents the Holy Spirit. Acacia grew plentifully in the desert and symbolizes humility. Gold represents deity, and the bread symbolizes the twelve tribes of Israel, the twelve disciples, and Jesus, who is the Bread of Life in John 6:35. Frankincense was a gift brought to Jesus by the Magi. It is white and represents purity. Frankincense was also used in the embalming process. Blue and purple cloths indicated royalty. Red symbolizes the blood, and the sheepskin represents the sacrificial lamb, Jesus.

Paul wrote to the Philippian church:

And if my lifeblood is, so to speak, to be poured out over your faith, which I am offering up to God as a sacrifice—that is, if I am to die for you—even then I will be glad ... (Philippians 2:17, TLB)

Paul was totally committed to his life in Christ, and his desire was for all people to give their hearts to the Lord. In the end, Paul did give up his life, but he looked forward to going to heaven to receive his reward from his Lord. He tells "... *to present your bodies a living and holy sacrifice, acceptable to God, which is your spiritual service of worship*" (Romans 12:1b, NASB). Some early churches were putting to much emphasis on spiritual gifts and not enough on how they were living for the Lord. He wanted them to be willing to be poured out in service to the Lord, like he was. So shall we.

Day Sixty-Five

BROKEN BREAD AND POURED-OUT WINE (PART TWO)

While they were eating, Jesus took some bread, and after
a blessing, He broke it and gave it to the disciples, and
said, "Take, eat; this is My body." And when he had
taken the cup and given thanks, He gave it to them,
saying, "Drink from it, all of you; for this is My
blood of the covenant, which is poured out
for many for forgiveness of sins."
(Matthew 26:26–31, NASB)

What does it mean to be broken bread and poured out wine before the Lord? Are we at the point of total surrender, and are we willing to do whatever the Lord requires of us? When we pray, can we say like Jesus did to His Father in heaven "*Your will be done*" (Matthew 6:10a, NASB)? Are we willing to serve where He leads us? Do we pour out our love on others who may be unloved and unlovely? Have we offered all of ourselves, our time, talents, and abilities to Him? Are we willing to share the story of Jesus with unbelievers? Are we thankful that Jesus poured out His life for us?

Jesus said: "*So you cannot become My disciple without giving up everything you own*" (Luke 14:33, NLT). Jesus gave all He had, and serving Him is a way of thanking Him for His broken body and poured-out blood. Throughout the centuries, Christians have been martyred for serving the Lord, and in some countries today people are being killed for loving Jesus. We in the Western world have not yet had to make the choice of life or death for Jesus. Our choice is to do what is required of us, which is to give Him our all—especially our hearts.

We know that grapes are just grapes until they are put into a wine press, squeezed, and crushed, all in the process of becoming the sweet-smelling aroma of wine that is then poured out on the altar of God. Once we tell the Lord we're ready to be poured out, He will reveal Himself to us.

Day Sixty-Six

BATTLES FOR OUR MIND

Our enemy, the devil, wants to destroy us spiritually, emotionally, and physically, and he uses our emotions against us. Our battles are won or lost in our minds. The devil started his work in the Garden of Eden when he played with Eve's mind and she ate the forbidden fruit. When God asked her what she had done, she said "*The serpent deceived me...*" (Genesis 3:13), or "*tricked me*" (TLB). The devil wanted to destroy Adam and Eve's relationship with God, and he did. They were cast out of the garden.

"*For our struggle is not against flesh and blood, but against the rulers, against the authorities, against the powers of this dark world and against the spiritual forces of evil in the heavenly realms*" (Ephesians 6:12). We are battling against the devil and his demons. When they attack us emotionally, we can get to a point in the battle where we feel unloved, unworthy, unhappy, and ungrateful. Then we feel isolated, abandoned, lonely, and rejected. It's easy to let the devil's garbage run through our minds and make us ungrateful to God. Satan wants us to blame God for all our troubles and become bitter and angry against Him.

Physically, the battle can be costly. War is stressful, and when we stress out and worry, we can't sleep or eat and eventually symptoms of a failing body appear. The devil uses stress to bring about aches, pains, and diseases. Stress can cause heart attacks! We win when we read and believe God's Word. Jesus tells us: "*Here on earth you will have many trials and sorrows; but cheer up, for I have overcome the world*" (John 16:33b, TLB). Satan only has as much power as our minds give him. He has already been defeated by the cross, and he loves to torment us. John tells us that "*… he who is in you is greater than he who is in the world*" (1 John 4:4b, NKJV).

We win when we "*… use God's mighty weapons, not those made by men, to knock down the devil's strongholds*" (2 Corinthians 10:4, TLB). We win when we "*Put on all of God's armor so that you will be able stand firm against all strategies of the devil*" (Ephesians 6:11, NLT).

Day Sixty-Seven

BATTLES FOR OUR MIND (PART TWO)

David writes: "*Trust in him* [God] *at all times, you people; pour out your hearts to Him …*" (Psalm 62:8a). The Lord wants us to trust Him for the victory. There really are only two choices: we can roll over, give up, and drown in self-pity, or we can trust that God will help us and become victors.

"*In every battle you will need faith as your shield to stop the fiery arrows aimed at you by Satan*" (Ephesians 6:16, TLB). Satan is on the hunt to "kill and destroy" our relationship with the Lord. He hunts us anytime, anywhere, and in every area of our lives. Battles are won on our knees, but Satan can make us believe that we are losing the war when our prayers seem to get lost in the air. We have a secret weapon, however—the Holy Spirit.

And the Holy Spirit helps us in our weakness. For example, we don't know what God wants us to pray for. But the Holy Spirit prays for us with groanings that cannot be expressed in words. And the Father who knows all hearts knows what the Spirit is saying, for

the Spirit pleads for us believers in harmony with God's own will.
(Romans 8:26–27, NLT)

Jesus won His battle with Satan in the wilderness after being tempted for forty days when He quoted scripture. Satan left Him, and angels came and attended Him (Matthew 4:4–11). Let's not fight the battle on our own strength. We can have the same power and strength as Jesus—we just need to ask. When the devil leaves and the fight is over, let's be thankful for the victory and praise and worship our Holy God. "*Therefore, since we are receiving a kingdom that cannot be shaken, let us be thankful, and so worship God acceptably with reverence and awe*" (Hebrews 12:28). Praise and worship heal our souls.

Roger Bennett was a southern gospel singer who wrote a song called, "I Read the Back of the Book and We Win." Revelation 20:10a confirms that: "*And the devil who deceived them* [people] *was thrown into the lake of fire and brimstone ...*" (NASB).

I heard a story about a man who viewed a large, framed picture displayed in a museum in a city in Europe. It was a picture of a chess game. The man studied it for a long time and finally said, "The king still has one more move." Our King Jesus has one more move, and Satan is going to a place where there will be torment day and night forever and ever (Revelation 20:10b).

Day Sixty-Eight

A Restoration Project

Restoration is like taking a trip. You can't get to where you're going if you stay where you are! *"I pray that from His glorious, unlimited resources he will empower you with inner strength through his Spirit"* (Ephesians 3:16, NLT). God sent Jesus to save us from our sins, and Jesus sent the Holy Spirit to restore us and make us new.

"… I will sing of your strength, in the morning I will sing of your love; for you are my fortress, my refuge in times of trouble. You are my strength, I sing praise to you …" (Psalm 59:16–17a). Gospel music has played a large part in my restoration process. When we sing praises to the Lord, He reciprocates with healing.

"And the God of all grace, who called you to his eternal glory in Christ, after you have suffered a little while, will himself restore you and make you strong, firm and steadfast" (1 Peter 5:10). When we're in a broken condition, we often wonder, "Will this ever end? Will I ever be whole again?" The answer is, "Yes." Our emotions can be healed, and we can be fully restored to a healthy mind and spirit. When we realize that we are not on God's respirator anymore but are breathing on our own, full recovery is ours.

"Those who live in the shelter of the Most High will find rest in the shadow of the Almighty" (Psalm 91:1, NLT). I have heard it said that for restoration we need to call 911—and Psalm 91:1 confirms that. With God as our 911 operator, we will be rescued.

"Therefore we do not lose heart. Though outwardly we are wasting away, yet inwardly we are being renewed day by day" (2 Corinthians 4:16). Sometimes we are wasting away on the inside but outwardly we don't show it. I received a note from a friend, Lorna, that said: "You are peaceful, and meekly go about your day without ever showing the outside world the pain you carry. Know that God has something special for you …" That note was a blessing and helped me realize that pain will end and the race to restoration can be won.

"Do you not know that in a race all the runners run, but only one gets the prize?" (1 Corinthians 9:24a). We run the race of life that has many obstacles, but we don't give up and quit running—because the prize is emotional healing and restoration. When there is nothing left there is God, our coach, cheering us on.

Day Sixty-Nine

LET GO, MOVE ON

Everyone has had things happen in the past that are unjust and unfair, but we are to take our eyes off the past, walk ahead with the Lord, and trust that He knows what He's doing in our lives—and move on. "*Trust in the Lord with all your heart and do not lean on your own understanding. In all your ways acknowledge Him, and He will make your paths straight*" (Proverbs 3:5–6, NASB). We need to turn the past over to the Lord, and He will guide our future. Let's not hold on to the past so tightly that we can't trust His plans for our lives. When held on to, the past can hold us captive and destroy us.

Paul says, "*… but I focus all on this one thing: Forgetting the past and looking forward to what lies ahead*" (Philippians 3:13, NLT). He had been on a mission to kill as many Christians as he could. When he turned his past over to Jesus, he let go of it. Then his main mission was to know the Lord intimately and to tell as many people as he could about Jesus and the cross. He let go and moved on to great things. Much of the New Testament was written by Paul, who found God's peace for his life. The Lord will use us when we move on. "*And the peace of God, which transcends all understanding, will guard your hearts and your minds* *in Christ Jesus*" (Philippians 4:7). God's peace will keep our thoughts off the past. When we totally trust Him, we can let go and move on.

I read a little article written by Ann Cetas titled, "Good Riddance."

On December 28th, 2008, the people of New York were invited to write on a sheet of paper, all their bad memories and hurts from the year, and bring them to Times Square where an industrial shredder would shred their lists. The shredded papers were thrown into a dumpster and hauled away. Hundreds came.[10]

We can do the same. Write down all the junk of our past, shred it, put it in the trash, and haul it away or recycle it into something new and exciting: "*Forget the former things; do not dwell on the past*" (Isaiah 43:18).

Getting stuck in the past is like walking into quicksand. It will suck us under and destroy personal relationships, our testimony, and our intimacy with the Lord. Don't get pulled under. Grab the Lord's hand, and He will pull us out of the hole of the past. Let's not look back to where God brought us from.

---

[10] Anne Cetas, "Good Riddance!" [*Our Daily Bread*] [https://odb.org/2009/12/27/good-riddance/].

Day Seventy

EAGLES' WINGS

Eagles are mentioned throughout the Bible. They are a fascinating bird, and their behavior patterns can be paralleled to our walk with the Lord. Eaglet babies are born with soft, fluffy feathers that, as they grow, are replaced with strong flying feathers. Once the flying feathers are developed, the mother eagle enrolls them in flying school. She leaves the nest and hovers over it until the eaglets start to flap their wings to imitate her. Next, she puts them on the crook of her wings and flies around the nest. Slowly she tips her wings until the babies begin to fall off. She watches them, and if they can't fly, she soars underneath them and catches them on her wings. If it's time to leave the nest and they still can't fly, she pokes holes in the bottom of the nest and tears it apart with her beak. The eagles are forced to leave and fly on their own.

When we start our walk with the Lord we are like the baby eaglets. As we develop spiritually, we use our flying feathers to learn how to fly for the Lord. We need to watch and imitate Him as He hovers over us and shows us the way to live. As He gently tips us off His wings, we can be assured that He will catch us if we need more instruction before we become mature and strong.

"*Like an eagle that stirs up its nest, That hovers over it's young, He* [God] *spread His wings and caught them. He carried them on His pinions* [feathers]" (Deuteronomy 32:11, NASB). Although this verse refers to the Israelites, God remains the same. His love never changes. Sometimes we get too comfortable in our nest, so God has to "stir up the nest" to get us to do what He asks of us. Like with the eaglets, the bottom has to drop out before we move.

"*But those who wait on the Lord Shall renew their strength; They shall mount up with wings like eagles, They shall run and not be weary, They shall walk and not faint*" (Isaiah 40:31, NKJV). "Waiting on the Lord is the patient expectation that God will fulfill His promises in His Word and strengthen us to rise above life difficulties. It means to completely trust in God." God never sleeps. He never becomes weary, and He won't faint. He walked the road to Calvary and He didn't give up and say He couldn't do it. He had the strength of His Father to help Him endure.

Day Seventy-One
EAGLES' WINGS (PART TWO)

I have an abundance of notes in my journal about eagles, so I hope you find them as intriguing as I do. They're strong, graceful, and swift. Their characteristics are unmatched by any other bird. Eagles can look directly into the sun because their eyes have filters. Our eyes don't need filters to look at the Son of God. We can look at His beauty and don't need protection to see Him.

When a storm approaches, the eagle won't seek shelter but will head into the storm with spread wings. The storm then carries it to the heights and safety. When we're in a storm we want to run and hide, not face it head on. We forget we belong to the Creator of the storm. If we trust Him and give Him the darkness of the storm, He'll help us soar above it.

Television evangelist Joyce Meyer spoke once about eagles on *Joyce Meyer Enjoying Everyday Living*. She explained that when a male and female eagle do their courtship, one of the tests is to lock their talons together, fly way up into the sky, and then drop through the air; she on the bottom. The male eagle will not let her go, even if it means he will die. To me, this is a picture of Jesus. He did not, and will not, let us go, which He proved when He took our place on the cross. He died so that we could live.

Another example Joyce used was that when eagles get old, they fly high up to the cleft of the rocks; pull out their feathers and wait forty days for new feathers to grow in. They don't move, they just sit there and wait. Because I'm a senior, the story of the old eagle pulling out its feathers and waiting for new ones amazes me. "*They will still bear fruit in old age …*" (Psalm 92:14a). Old age shouldn't keep us from flying. After all, we have the Master instructor still guiding us. When we seniors get our new feathers, we need to teach the young how to fly with the Lord.

God teaches and instructs us when we have fluffy feathers all the way up to feather replacement in old age. Aren't we blessed?

Day Seventy-Two

THE FREEDOM OF FORGIVENESS

*You were dead because of your sins and because your
sinful nature was not yet cut away. Then God made you
alive with Christ, for he forgave all our sins. He canceled
the record of the charges against us and took it
away by nailing it to the cross.*
(Colossians 2:13–14, NLT)

Our sins were nailed to the cross with Jesus, so we can go directly
to Him for forgiveness. When God gave us the gift of forgiveness,
He asked that we forgive those who sin against us. We can never forget
the enormous price Jesus paid so we could be forgiven. "*As far as the east
is from the west, so far has He [Jesus] removed our transgressions from us*"
(Psalm 103:12, NKJV). When God forgives our sins, they are gone. He
gave us the example of forgiveness to follow, and we are called to obey.

Jesus said, "*If you forgive those who sin against you, your heavenly
Father will forgive you. But if you refuse to forgive others, your Father will
not forgive your sins*" (Matthew 6:14–15, NLT). It's easier to ask God to
forgive us than it is to forgive those who sinned against us, but Scripture
says to do it!

Peter wrote: "*He [Jesus] did not retaliate when he was insulted, nor
threaten revenge when he suffered. He left His case in the hands of God,
who always judges fairly*" (1 Peter 2:23, NLT). Many of us have a natural

instinct to retaliate. When we lash out in revenge, we lose. We need to let it go and let God, our Defender Judge, do what He has to do to win our case. With God as our lawyer, we can't lose.

"*Love prospers when a fault is forgiven, but dwelling on it separates close friends*" (Proverbs 17:9, NLT). We haven't forgiven if we continually find fault and speak of those faults to others. We haven't forgiven if we constantly bring up past hurts to anyone who will listen. We haven't forgiven if we want payback for the ones who sinned against us or if we want revenge. "*Do not take revenge, my dear friends, but leave room for God's wrath, for it is written: 'It is mine to avenge; I will repay,' says the Lord*" (Romans 12:19). It's plain to see—we are forgiven, and we need to forgive and let God work for justice on our behalf. "*And when you stand praying, if you hold anything against anyone, forgive him, so that your Father in heaven may forgive you your sins*" (Mark 11:25).

Day Seventy-Three

OUT OF THE MUD AND MIRE, I RISE

*"I waited patiently for the Lord; he turned
to me and heard my cry."*
(Psalm 40:1)

When I was a new Christian, way back in the late 1970s, a male singer and evangelist from the U.S.A. came to our church for special meetings. I don't remember his name or what he looked like, but I remember his story. Psalm 40:1–3 was his text that weekend. His wife had left him, and he was devastated, but these three verses helped him survive.

I remember feeling bad for him because his story was sad; however, the verse he stressed the most was verse two: "*He lifted me out of the slimy pit, out of the mud and mire; he set my feet on a rock and gave me a firm place to stand.*" The NLT says "*… He set my feet on solid ground and steadied me as I walked along.*" I find it ironic that some thirty-five plus years later I'm writing about the same subject. I don't know how his story ended, but mine is Psalm 40:3a: "*He* [God] *put a new song in my mouth, a song of praise to our God …*" (NASB). "*O Lord my God, you have performed many wonders for us. Your plans for us are too numerous to list*" (Psalm 40:5a, NLT).

When we're back on our feet we need to remember all the good things the Lord has done for us and thank Him for all He has planned.

"... I finally understand—you don't require burnt offerings or sin offerings" (Psalm 40:6, NLT); *"... I take joy in doing your will, my God, for your instructions are written on my heart"* (Psalm 40:8b, NLT). God wants us to get rid of the muck in our lives, leave any rituals behind, and give Him our love, praise, and will. *"I [David] have not kept this good news of your justice hidden in my heart; I have talked about your faithfulness and saving power. I have told everyone ... of your unfailing love and faithfulness"* (Psalm 40:10, NLT); *"But may all who search for you be filled with joy and gladness in you. May those who love your salvation repeatedly shout, 'The Lord is great!'"* (Psalm 40:16, NLT). Let's love and praise the Lord by sharing His love and goodness to all who need to get up out of the mud and mire. We need to remember, God is the Potter—He works with mud.

> *We are pressed on every side by troubles, but not crushed and broken. We are perplexed because we don't know why things happen as they do, but we don't give up and quit ... We get knocked down, but we get up again and keep going.* (2 Corinthians 4:8–9, TLB)

I read a quote once that said: "When we're down, lying on our backs in the mud and mire, that's the best position to look up to God." Let's look up, rise up, give our hearts and lives to the Lord, and He will give us a new song to sing.

Day Seventy-Four

PRESSED DOWN—SHAKEN TOGETHER

*This Melchizedek was king of the city of Salem [later
Jerusalem] and also a priest of God Most High. When
Abraham was returning home after winning a great
battle against the kings, Melchizedek met him and
blessed him. Then Abraham took a tenth of all he had
captured in battle and gave it to Melchizedek. The name
Melchizedek means "king of justice," and king of Salem
means "king of peace." There is no record of his father or
mother or any of his ancestors—no beginning or
end to his life. He remains a priest forever,
resembling the Son of God.*
(Hebrews 7:1–3, NLT)

Melchizedek is first mentioned in Genesis 14. "One of the most
mysterious people in the Bible is the king of peace, Melchizedek.
He appeared one day in the life of Abraham (then Abram) and was never
heard from again…"[11] "One theory of Melchizedek was that he was the
appearance of the preincarnate Christ in temporary bodily form."[12] That
was the first time the figure one-tenth was used.

---

[11] *Life Application Study Bible, NLT* (Wheaton, IL: Tyndale House Publishers, Inc.,
1996), 29.
[12] Ibid. 27.

You must each decide in your heart how much to give. And don't give reluctantly or in response to pressure. "For God loves a person who gives cheerfully." And God will generously provide all you need. Then you will always have everything you need and plenty left over to share with others. (2 Corinthians 9:7–8, NLT)

If we tithe expecting God to bless us, it won't happen. But if we tithe with the attitude of thankfulness for all the Lord has given to us, He in turn will bless us, *"pressed down, shaken together"* (Luke 6:38).

"You must not hold anything back when you give me offerings from your crops and your wine …" (Exodus 22:29a, NLT). Giving God the first part of our earnings demonstrates that He has first priority in our lives. Sometimes money is tight and we think our needs come first, but if we are faithful and give, He in return will "bless our socks off!"

Jesus said: *"Do not lay up for yourselves treasures on earth … but lay up for yourselves treasures in heaven … For where your treasure is, there your heart will be also"* (Matthew 6:19–21, NKJV). Let's give our tithes to God joyfully. *"… the purses of heaven never get old or develop holes …"* (Luke 12:33b, NLT). We will never lose God's blessing if we give willingly out of love. We can never out-give the Lord, because He owns it all—everything!

Day Seventy-Five

PRESSED DOWN—SHAKEN TOGETHER (PART TWO)

FROM "MY STORY" BY DUANE ASHTON[13]

My nephew Duane was in the process of transitioning from a thirty-three-year military career to civilian life. At that time his church, Washington Community Church, desired to lead their people into a growing relationship with Jesus. They recognized that, according to John 3:16, God gave His Son to us to bless us and show how we are to give from what we've been blessed with. At this particular point in his life, he'd completed a contract job and was waiting for his last cheque, and he was questioning if there would be another job opportunity. This created an internal debate. What would they do until he got another job? Would they be able to eat and pay bills? The question became: "Do we tithe or do we eat?" He was obedient and payed their tithe plus an offering, and God blessed them. He got another job opportunity and when his cheque came, it was ten times the amount of the tithe.

Malachi admonishes the Israelites for not tithing, but he says there will be blessings if they do:

---

[13] Used by permission from Duane Ashton.

"Bring the whole tithe into the storehouse … Test Me in this," says the Lord Almighty, "and see if I will not throw open the floodgates of heaven and pour out so much blessing that there will not be room enough to store it." (Malachi 3:10–11)

God promises that when you give a tithe willingly, He will give it back to you.

Give, and it will be given to you. They will pour into your lap a good measure—pressed down, shaken together, and running over. For by your standard of measure it will be measured to you in return (Luke 6:38, NASB).

Day Seventy-Six

IN SILENCE—LISTEN AND WAIT

*"O Lord … Do not turn a deaf ear to me. For if You are
silent, I might as well give up and die."*
(Psalm 28:1, NLT)

What does it mean when God is silent? It doesn't mean that He's not there or that He's not listening … He might just be trying to bring us to an intimacy with Him that can't be attained if we aren't silent before Him. It could also be that He wants us to quietly stand in awe of Him. Maybe He wants to reveal a truth to us that we're too busy to see. Jesus said:

So be sure to pay attention to how you hear. To those who listen to my teaching, more understanding will be given. But to those who are not listening, even what they think they understand will be taken away from them. (Luke 8:18, NLT)

God speaks to us through His Word. We learn by reading it and by listening to it spoken to us by teachers and preachers; however, if we don't grow in wisdom and knowledge, we become stagnant in our walk with Him and could forget the truths we've learned in the past.

"Wait for the Lord; Be strong, and let your heart take courage; Yes, wait for the Lord" (Psalm 27:14, NASB). It's hard to wait for anything in this

world of instant everything. God, however, has His own timetable and schedule, as we read about in 2 Peter 3:8: "*But do not forget this one thing, dear friends: With the Lord a day is like a thousand years, and a thousand years are like a day.*" We find it hard to wait for God to answer us when we bring our prayer requests to Him, and He pushes the pause button. We need to remember His timing and believe He will speak to us when He feels we're ready to hear what He has to say.

"*Don't be impatient for the Lord to act! Keep traveling steadily along his pathway and in due season he will honor you with every blessing ...*" (Psalm 37:34, TLB). Let's let God do what He has planned for us ... when He sees fit. He wants the very best for us, His children, so we need to give Him all the time He needs to work out the perfect plan for us.

I found this little nugget of wisdom in my notes. SILENT and LISTEN have exactly the same letters in them. That tells me that when I'm silent before the Lord and listen to what He has to say to me, I will be blessed and surrounded by His presence in the stillness.

Day Seventy-Seven

HELLO GOD, LET'S TALK

Thousands of pages have been written about prayer over the years, and a multitude of prayers are written in the Bible, but "The Lord's Prayer" (Matthew 6:8–13) and the "Hight Priestly Prayer" John 17:1–26, prayed by Jesus, are spoken of the most. My focus here is on spending time getting to know the Lord through conversation with Him in the hope of understanding what speaking with Him means. In a human relationship, we get to know someone better by spending time with them and talking and listening to each other. As time passes, we develop an emotional intimacy with each other. So too is it with the Lord. He wants that same intimacy. Let's go into our prayer room and take Him with us.

Jesus said: "*But when you pray, go into your room, close the door and pray to your Father, who is unseen. Then your Father, who sees what is done in secret, will reward you*" (Matthew 6:6). Sometimes when we go into our prayer room to be with the Lord, our thoughts begin to wander and our minds go in all directions. We start thinking about what we need to do that day, or what bills we need to pay. At that point, we need to shut the emotional door of distractions, focus on the Lord, and learn to recognize His voice.

"My heart has heard you say, 'Come and talk with Me.' And My heart responds, 'Lord, I am coming'" (Psalm 27:8, NLT). "Talk with me" means conversation, a back and forth exchange, not "I'll talk and then I'll walk away." We say "Amen" and we're out the door.

In John 10:27, Jesus our Shepherd says that we, His sheep, His children, know His voice: *"My sheep recognize my voice, and I know them, and they follow me"* (TLB). The only way we recognize His voice is by spending time with Him. The more we let Him speak, the more we know His will for our daily lives.

The Holy Spirit was sent to help us in our prayer time. Many times we are so overcome by life's tragedies, we're unable to express our pain. Paul assures us that when our burdens are too great, the Holy Spirit intercedes for us: *"And the Holy Spirit helps us in our weakness. For example, we don't know what God wants us to pray for. But the Holy Spirit prays for us with groanings that cannot be expressed in words"* (Romans 8:26, NLT). When we're in our prayer room, it's as though we're standing on holy ground (Exodus 3:5).

Day Seventy-Eight
"The Time of the Lord's Favor Has Come"

As I pen this page, we're approaching Easter—the appropriate time to celebrate the favor of salvation given to us by the life, death, and resurrection of Jesus, our Lord and Savior. I searched the Bible and various other avenues to help me understand what the word "favor" really means. In the Old Testament, favor meant a blessing that involved protection, compassion, and mercy. I also learned that favor meant grace, honor, and forgiveness. A blessing was a sign of approval, love, and peace. In the New Testament, along with the Old Testament blessings, God favored us with His Son, Jesus. Our salvation through the cross was an unmerited, undeserved favor given out of love. By the grace of God and His Son, Jesus, we can be saved.

King David wasn't afraid to ask God to bless him with His favor. He wanted God's blessing in his many times of trouble: "*I sought Your favor with my whole heart; be merciful and gracious to me according to Your promise*" (Psalm 119:58, AMP); "*Send me a sign of your favor…*" (Psalm 86:17a, TLB). God always answered David with a blessing.

"*This is what the Lord says: 'In the time of my favor I will answer you, and in the day of salvation I will help you*" (Isaiah 49:8a) The Messiah was given to us as a sign of God's favor to all mankind. God was going to restore Israel, and it would come through His Son, Jesus. The time of the Lord's favor came with Jesus' birth in Bethlehem, the cross at Calvary, His resurrection, and His ascension back to heaven. As we give our lives to Jesus by asking Him to come into our hearts and forgive us, we are blessed with God's favor, because He loves us.

"*He has sent me* [Isaiah] *... to tell those who mourn that the time of God's favor to them has come ... To all who mourn ... he will give: beauty for ashes; Joy instead of mourning; praise instead of heaviness ...*" (Isaiah 61:1–3, TLB). Jesus fulfilled this prophecy hundreds of years later when He went into the synagogue at Nazareth, on the Sabbath, and unrolled the scroll to the place where it was written, by Isaiah "*... the time of the Lord's favor has come. He rolled up the scroll, handed it back to the attendant, and sat down ... Then he began to speak to them. 'The Scripture you've just heard has been fulfilled this very day!'*" (Luke 4: 19–21, NLT). Jesus our High Priest is the favor and righteousness of God given to us for our salvation through the forgiveness of sin.

Day Seventy-Nine

"The Time of the Lord's Favor Has Come"
(Part Two)

In his letter to the Ephesian church, Paul tells us that the Lord has favored us:

Now all praise to God for His wonderful kindness to us and his favor that he has poured out upon us because we belong to his dearly loved Son. So overflowing is His kindness toward us that he took away all our sins through the blood of his Son, by whom we are saved; and he has showered down upon us the richness of his grace—for how well He understands us and knows what is best for us at all times. (Ephesians 1:6–8, TLB)

But God is so rich in mercy; he loved us so much that even though we were spiritually dead and doomed by our sins, he gave us back our lives again when He raised Christ from the dead—only by His undeserved favor have we ever been saved. (Ephesians 2:4–5, TLB)

"God saved you by his grace when you believed. And you can't take credit for this; it is a gift from God" (Ephesians 2:8, NLT).

Paul said:

You know what I was like when I followed the Jewish religion—how I violently persecuted God's church. I did my best to destroy it ... But even before I was born, God choose me and called me by his marvelous grace ... (Galatians 1:13, 15, NLT)

Paul hated the Christians before he met Christ, and he had many killed. He was on a mission to Damascus, armed with a letter that would force the Christians there to go back to Jerusalem, where they would be put to death. But the Lord had other plans for Paul. Jesus met him on the road and showered him with mercy and favor that changed his life forever.

I [Paul] became a servant of this gospel by the gift of God's grace given me through the working of His power. Although I am less than the least of all the Lord's people, this grace was given me: to preach to the Gentiles the boundless riches of Christ. (Ephesians 3:7–8)

The Lord favored me, a Gentile, with the privilege of knowing Him intimately. He favored me with the truth of His Word. I am blessed to be called His child, His daughter. He has favored me with His Holy Spirit, and in turn I honor Him as I cry out in praise, "Holy, Holy, Holy." I covet His presence in my life.

Day Eighty

BETHLEHEM—BIRTH PLACE OF KINGS

Bethlehem, which means "Bread of Life," was only about six miles south of Jerusalem. It was a small farming community that had been blessed with bountiful crops. Once one of the oldest Christian communities in Judea, today Bethlehem is controlled by Arab Muslins. Their economy is strong partly because of the many tourists who are allowed to visit the birthplace of Jesus. Bethlehem has an interesting, God-planned history. Naomi, Ruth, and Boaz play an intricate part of the history, as do two kings: King David and King Jesus.

"*Boaz was the father of Obed. Obed was the father of Jesse. Jesse was the father of David*" (Ruth 4:21b–22, NLT). David would become king. He was born in Bethlehem and is in the genealogy of King Jesus, the Messiah.

"*… He* [God] *raised up David to be their king … and said, 'I have found David the son of Jesse, a man after My heart, who will do all My will'*" (Acts 13:22, NASB). David lived in Bethlehem and he was a shepherd to his father's sheep. Samuel was sent to Bethlehem to the house of Jesse to find a king, and David was anointed.

"So Jesse sent for him [David]. *He was dark and handsome, with beautiful eyes. And the Lord said* [to Samuel]; *'This is the one; anoint him.'"* (1 Samuel 16:12, NLT). Jesus was born in Bethlehem and is the shepherd of His Father's sheep. Both kings are ordained by God. Jesus is our kinsman redeemer.

"O Bethlehem Ephrathah, you are but a small Judean village, yet you will be the birthplace of my King [Jesus] *who is alive from everlasting ages past"* (Micah 5:2, TLB).

There is a line in a Korean Christmas carol that says: "Christmas shines with Easter glory, glory of eternity." At the foot of the manger stood the cross! Another powerful Christmas song is "Mary Did You Know?" It asks if Mary knew that when she kissed her baby she was kissing the face of God. Jesus was born God; He didn't grow up and become God.

Day Eighty-One

JERUSALEM—CITY OF GOD

The story of Jerusalem is tremendously important to Jewish history and continues in importance to Christianity and our world today. In Genesis 14 we're introduced to Melchizedek, the high priest and King of Salem, as he meets with and blesses Abraham. Salem would later become Jerusalem.

God loved Jerusalem and promised to live there.

> *This is what the Lord of Heaven's Armies says: "My love for Mount Zion is passionate and strong; I am consumed with passion for Jerusalem! And now the Lord says: I am returning to Mount Zion, and I will live in Jerusalem. Then Jerusalem will be called the Faithful City ... the Holy Mountain."* (Zechariah 8:2–3, NLT)

When King Solomon finished building the temple of the Lord, he said: "*This must be a magnificent Temple because our God is greater than all other gods. Not even the highest heavens can contain Him! So who am I to consider building a Temple for him ...*" (2 Chronicles 2:5–6, NLT). The temple is relevant to Christianity as it symbolizes the importance of God's presence and power.

The story of Jesus and Jerusalem began when He was young and it remained an intricate part of His life. When Jesus was twelve years old He went with His parents from Nazareth for the Passover in Jerusalem. People often traveled together in groups as protection against robbers. On the way home Jesus went missing, so His parents returned to Jerusalem and found Him in the Temple talking with the teachers. When asked why He'd done that to them, he said, *"Didn't you know I had to be in my Father's house ?"* (Luke 2:49). After that Jesus obeyed His parents and *"grew in wisdom and stature, and in favor with God and man"* (Luke 2:52). As an adult Jesus spent many days in Jerusalem, teaching and attending all the major Jewish festivals. He would always attend the Passover festival.

Jesus told His disciples that when they got to Jerusalem, He would be betrayed and handed over to the Romans. *"They will mock him, spit on him, flog him with a whip, and kill him, but after three days he will rise again"* (Mark 10:34, NLT). This was the third time Jesus told them what would happen, but they didn't understand.

Then I [John] saw a new heaven and a new earth; for the first heaven and the first earth passed away ... And I saw the holy city, new Jerusalem, coming down out of heaven from God ... And I heard a loud voice from the throne, saying, "Behold the tabernacle of God is among men, and He will dwell among them... and God Himself will be among them ... " (Revelation 21:1–3, NASB)

The Lord is coming again, as He said.

Day Eighty-Two

In Remembrance of Me

Luke seems to indicate an urgency for Jesus to get to Jerusalem. "…
he moved steadily onward toward Jerusalem" (Luke 9:51, TLB); "…
teaching as he went, always pressing on toward Jerusalem" (Luke 13:22,
NLT). He moved steadily onward toward Jerusalem with an iron will.
Jesus pushed ahead, knowing what was awaiting Him there.

Upon arriving at Jerusalem, Jesus sent two of His disciples to a
village close by to bring a colt back. All they needed to say was, "*The
Lord needs it*" (Luke 19:31). Jesus rode the donkey over cloaks that the
crowd had thrown on the ground. "*They took palm branches and went out
to meet him, shouting, 'Hosanna! Blessed is he who comes in the name of
the Lord!'*" (John 12:12–13). When the Pharisees told Jesus to quiet the
crowd, He told them that if the crowd was quiet, "*the stones will cry out*"
(Luke 19:40, NASB).

Let's just stop here and imagine what would happen if the crowd
was quiet. In my mind, I see the rocks as a choir of angels just praising
the Lord. I can almost hear them!

Jesus knew what was in store for Jerusalem in the future, and when
He saw it, "… *he wept over it*" (Luke 19:41a). Twice while Jesus was

teaching in the temple He threw the merchants' tables over and said to them, "*My house will be a house of prayer*" (Luke 19:46).

The Pharisees were looking for a way to kill Jesus, so when Judas Iscariot offered up Jesus, they knew they finally had Him. They gladly paid the thirty pieces of silver (Matthew 26:14–16). Jesus told His disciples "*I have eagerly desired to eat this Passover with you before I suffer*" (Luke 22:15). After supper, He "*poured water into a basin, and began to wash the disciples' feet and to wipe them with the towel he had around him*" (John 13:5, TLB). How He loved His disciples! (Imagine God washing our feet—how humbling.)

> ... *on the same night in which He was betrayed took bread; and when He had given thanks, He broke it and said, "Take, eat; this is My body which is broken for you; do this in remembrance of Me." In the same manner He also took the cup after supper, saying, "This cup is the new covenant in My blood ..."* (1 Corinthians 11:23–26, NKJV)

The new covenant is to love one another as Christ has loved us (John 13:34–35). When they had sung a hymn, they went out to the Mount of Olives (Matthew 26:30). The Lord's time of agony was about to begin.

Day Eighty-Three
THE ROAD TO CALVARY

When Jesus and His disciples arrived at Gethsemane, Jesus knew what He had to endure to fulfill what the prophets had written about Him. He had read the scrolls and saw the blood and felt the pain.. *"… They have pierced my hands and feet. I can count all my bones. My enemies stare at me and gloat. They divide my garments among themselves and throw dice [cast lots] for my clothing"* (Psalm 22:16b–18, NLT); *"My back is covered with cuts, as if a farmer had plowed long furrows"* (Psalm 129:3, NLT); *"I give my back to the whip, and my cheeks to those who pull out the beard. I do not hide from shame—they spit in my face"* (Isaiah 50:6, TLB); *"…They shall see My Servant beaten and bloodied, so disfigured one would scarcely know it was a person standing there …"* (Isaiah 52:15, TLB).

Jesus needed to talk to His Father about His suffering, and He wanted His disciples to pray with Him; after all, He loved them so much … surely they would stay awake and pray. Jesus left His disciples and went a little farther ahead to talk with His Father, *"… and fell face down on the ground, and prayed, 'My Father! If it is possible, let this cup be taken away from me. But I want your will, not mine'"* (Matthew 26:39, TLB).

Jesus went back to check on His disciples, and they were asleep. A third time He went back to talk to His Father, because He didn't have enough human strength to face being separated from His Father while carrying our sins on the cross. *"And being in agony, He prayed more earnestly. Then His sweat became like great drops of blood falling down to the ground"* (Luke 22:44, NKJV). He finally had peace in His soul, and *"… he humbled himself even further, going so far as to die a criminal's death on a cross"* (Philippians 2:8, TLB).

Jesus also knew that Peter would deny Him three times before He was crucified, and He felt the pain of betrayal (Luke 22:34, NIV). Just then *"… a crowd came up, and the man who was called Judas … was leading them … He approached Jesus to kiss him"* (Luke 22:47). The kiss of death! This too was no surprise to Jesus: *"Even my best friend [Judas], the one I trusted completely, the one who shared my food, has turned against me"* (Psalm 41:9, NLT). At that point, *"… all the disciples deserted Him and fled"* (Matthew 26:56b, TLB).

Jesus saw us and our sin, and He knew that dying for us would give us a new way to heaven. He gave His blood, His life, for our souls. Let's not desert Him too. Let's go the rest of the way with Him.

Day Eighty-Four

THE THORNS AND THE CROSS

The rest of the way to the cross with Jesus is brutal with unbelievable suffering. After Judas betrayed Jesus, and His followers deserted Him, He was seized, bound, and led away by the soldiers and the mob that came with them. Jesus was taken before the high priest, Caiaiphas. When asked if He was the Christ, the Son of God, Jesus answered, "Yes, it is as you say." The high priest tore his clothes, yelling, "Blasphemy," and all there said He should die. They blindfolded Him, spit in His face, and struck Him with their fists. Others slapped Him and told Him to tell them who hit Him. All through this, Jesus was silent.

The next morning it was decided to kill Jesus, but it needed to be presented to Pilate, the governor. When Judas realized that Jesus was sentenced to death, he threw the thirty pieces of silver on the temple floor and went out and hung himself. Jesus was bound again and sent to Herod, where He was ridiculed and mocked when they put a royal robe on Him. Sent back to Pilate, Jesus was asked if He was the Christ, the Son of God, to which he again replied, "Yes, it is as you say."

Pilate offered to release Jesus, as it was the custom at Passover to release one prisoner. The mob chose to free Barabbas, a notorious prisoner, and crucify Jesus. Pilate was afraid, and he knew Jesus was innocent, so he washed his hands in a basin of water to show that the blood of Jesus wasn't on him. He sent Jesus to the palace, where the soldiers stripped Him and put a scarlet (purple) robe on Him. They twisted a crown of thorns together and set it on His head. Then they put a staff in His right hand and knelt before Him and mocked Him: "Hail, King of the Jews." After spitting on Him, they used the staff to beat on His head repeatedly, and the blood began to drip from His brow. Finally, they put His own clothes back on Him.

Pilate had ordered Jesus to be flogged with Roman whips, so the soldiers tied Jesus to a pole and hurled whips that had metal, spear-shaped ends on them. Wham! His back was cut. Wham! More cuts, and His blood began to flow. Wham! Wham! His back was ripped open, and His blood ran down to the ground. Finally, the beating stopped and He was led out to be crucified. He was unrecognizable. He was beaten to a pulp. Yet He was silent.

Day Eighty-Five
THE THORNS AND THE CROSS (PART TWO)

Weak from being beaten and whipped, Jesus was forced to carry His own cross. As He struggled to walk the road to Calvary, another Old Testament prophecy was fulfilled. Two goats were brought into the Tent of Meeting, where one goat was sacrificed and its blood was sprinkled on the other goat. After an atonement ceremony, the live goat was sent into the wilderness, carrying the sins of the people (Leviticus 16:3–26). Calvary was outside the city of Jerusalem, and Jesus personally carried our sins into the wilderness, where He gave his life.

Jesus faltered as He carried His heavy load, so a man named Simon, who was just passing through, was forced to carry the cross to the top of the hill. Many of the bystanders were weeping and wailing, and many were cheering. The noise was deafening, yet there was a quiet calm that could only come from Jesus. At the top of the hill called Golgotha, meaning The Skull, the cross was ready for Jesus. They laid Him down on the cross and stretched out His arms, one arm to the left and one arm to the right. With a hammer and nails they hammered the nails into His body. He bore all our sins as they hammered the nails. Bang! Murder, abuse. Bang! Adultery. Bang! Fornication. Then they went to

His feet. Bang! Thief. Bang! Drunkard. Bang! Homosexual relations and all the remaining sins of the people (1 Corinthians 6:10; Deuteronomy 5:11–21; Exodus 20:7–17). When He was firmly nailed, the cross was dropped into the prepared hole, and His flesh ripped more as the weight of His body was put on His hands and feet. There was so much blood!

A sign reading, JESUS OF NAZARETH, THE KING OF THE JEWS, was written in Aramaic, Latin, and Greek and nailed above His head on the cross. As prophesied, the solders divided His clothes and cast lots for His seamless garment. Jesus hung there beaten and bloodied, "unrecognizable."

As the hours passed, Jesus spoke several times before He died. He said, *"Father, forgive them, for they do not know what they are doing"* (Luke 23:34). Jesus' first words were about forgiveness. Have we asked Jesus to forgive our sins? Have we forgiven those who hurt and rejected us? Jesus did, so too can we!

Two thieves were crucified beside Jesus. One scoffed and the other defended Jesus, who had done no wrong. Then Jesus said to him, *"I tell you the truth, today you will be with me in Paradise"* (Luke 23:43). This is a solemn promise.

Day Eighty-Six

THE THORNS AND THE CROSS (PART THREE)

When Jesus saw His mother standing with Mary Magdalene, some other women, and His disciple, John, Jesus said to His mother: *"Dear woman, here is your son"* (John 19:26, NLT). To John He said, *"Here is your mother"* (John 19:27, NLT). From that time on, John took care of Mary, the mother of Jesus. Jesus made sure that she would be cared for.

Jesus cried out, *"My God, my God, why have you forsaken Me?"* (Matthew 27:46). These were the most painful words that Jesus spoke on the cross, because His Father could not look at sin, and His Son had all our sins on Him. Jesus felt the sting of rejection from His own Father. Jesus had to be rejected so that we could be accepted. When the sky was dark for three hours, I wonder if it wasn't partly because God couldn't look any longer on the agony of His Son.

When Jesus said, "I thirst," He was given sour wine on a hyssop branch. Hyssop was used to spread the blood of the Passover lamb over the doorposts of the Israelites homes when the angel of death passed over on the night they were delivered from Egypt. Jesus is the Passover lamb that shed His blood for us.

When Jesus said "It is finished," He was saying that He had finished what His Father sent Him to earth to do. Animal sacrifices were finished. His death was payment for our sins. The only way sin can be forgiven now is through the cross, where the devil was defeated.

Jesus said, "*'Father, into your hands I commit my spirit.' When he had said this, he breathed his last*" (Luke 23:46). One day we will breathe our last, and if we have been forgiven, Jesus will welcome us to heaven with open arms.

The soldiers had to make sure that Jesus was dead, because his body had to be taken down before the Sabbath. If He wasn't dead, his legs would be broken to speed up the process. When the soldiers thrust a spear into Jesus' side, blood and water came out. Jesus was dead, fulfilling the prophecy that "*not one of them* [His bones] *will be broken*" (Psalm 34:20, NLT).

This account was taken from Matthew 26–27; Mark 14–15; Luke 22–23; John 18–19.

Day Eighty-Seven

AFTER THE CROSS

When Jesus "gave up His Spirit," there was no mistake— Jesus was the Son of God.

At that moment the curtain in the sanctuary of the Temple was torn in two, from top to bottom. The earth shook, rocks split apart, and tombs opened. The bodies of many godly men and women who had died were raised from the dead. (Matthew. 27:51–53, NLT)

Later these saints were seen in Jerusalem by many people. The tearing of the curtain between the Holy Place and the Most Holy Place in the temple is significant, as it abolished the old system of the high priest going into the Most Holy Place once a year to ask forgiveness for the sins of the people. When the curtain tore, Jesus became the High Priest, allowing us to go directly to Him.

Before Jesus died, the devil had the power of death. But between the time of His death and resurrection, Jesus victoriously took the keys away from the devil: "*I am the living one. I died, but look—I am alive forever*

173

and ever! And I hold the keys of death and the grave [Hades]" (Revelation 1:18, NLT).

Jesus' disciples had all deserted Him, so a man named Joseph from Arimathea asked Pilate for His body. He and Nicodemus wrapped Jesus in burial spices and put Him in a new tomb where no body had ever been laid before (John 19:38–42, NIV). Then they sealed the grave with a large rock.

On the first day of the week, early in the morning, Mary Magdalene and some other women went to the tomb to anoint Jesus with spices. When they got there, there was an earthquake, and an angel rolled the stone away and sat on it. He said, "*He in not here; he has risen*" (Matthew 28:6). They were instructed to go tell the disciples to meet Jesus in Galilee. The women told the disciples that Jesus was alive, and Peter and John went to the tomb to see for themselves (John 20:1–9).

Later, Mary Magdalene returned to the garden that was close to the tomb. She was crying because Jesus wasn't in the tomb. Someone was standing behind her, but she didn't recognize that it was Jesus. She thought it was the gardener, but when He said her name, she went toward Him. He said to her, "*Don't touch me ... for I haven't yet ascended to the Father. But go find my brothers and tell them that I ascend to my Father and your Father, my God and your God*" (John 20:17, TLB).

Day Eighty-Eight
AFTER THE CROSS (PART TWO)

That same evening as the disciples were meeting behind closed doors, Jesus appeared to them. Doubting Thomas, who hadn't seen Jesus yet, didn't believe it really was Him, so Jesus said, "*Put your finger into my hands. Put your hand into my side. Don't be faithless any longer. Believe!*" (John 20:27, TLB).

Recently, I was shown something about these scriptures that I'd never seen before. In the morning Jesus told Mary not to touch Him, yet that evening He told Thomas to touch Him. What happened that day that changed everything? He ascended to the Father, and it sounds like He was given a different body. I think it's similar to the body we will be given when we see the Father. What a nugget! Before I move on … The body of Jesus being raised from the dead is another fulfillment of prophecy written by David: "*For you will not leave my soul among the dead or allow your holy one to rot in the grave*" (Psalms 16:10, NLT).

After Jesus was resurrected He was seen by many people and He visited His disciples many times. During one meeting, He said, "*As the Father has sent me, even so I am sending you. Then he breathed on them and told them, 'Receive the Holy Spirit*" (John 20:21–22, TLB).

He commanded them not to depart from Jerusalem, but to wait for the Promise of the Father, saying that they would be baptized by the Holy Spirit within a few days ... *"you shall receive power when the Holy Spirit has come upon you ... and you shall be witnesses to Me ... to the end of the earth"* Acts 1:8, NKJV).

> *And Jesus came and spoke to them, saying, "All authority has been given to Me in heaven and on earth. Go therefore and make disciples of all the nations, baptizing them in the name of the Father and of the Son and of the Holy Spirit, teaching them to observe all things that I have commanded you; and lo, I am with you always, even to the end of the age. Amen [so be it]."* (Matthew 28:18–20, NKJV)

"Now when He had spoken these things, while they watched, He was taken up, and a cloud received Him out of their sight" (Acts 1:9, NKJV). Let's not forget that Jesus said He is coming again. And I believe!

Day Eighty-Nine

AT THE MOUNTAIN

As we journey through life we learn many things. We learn that the past can either destroy us or we can live victoriously because of the grace and love of God. When we go through the refining fire of God, we come out a beautiful diamond. Praising and worshiping the Lord restores our souls. Intimacy with the Lord requires spending time in His presence and in His Word. Friends leave, but the Lord never leaves. He stays right here with us.

We can be thankful in *all* things, good or bad, happy or sad. God's timing is perfect. He's never ahead or behind. He's right where He should be. When heartbreak brings us to our knees, we kneel at the feet of Jesus. God's plans and ours aren't always the same, but His are best.

God helps us overcome our fear of being alone, as He's always with us. If all we have left is the Lord, He is enough. Obedience is better that rebellion. God disciplines rebellion and blesses obedience. To trust the Lord we have to give Him control of every area of our lives. To forgive we need to let go of the past and go to the other side of hurt with Jesus. Baggage is a blessing to a traveler but a hindrance to a happy home.

The more time we spend with the Lord, the easier it is to live for Him. We need to be an example and walk the road of righteousness. Waiting for the Lord to act on our behalf is different than waiting before the Lord. We're never too old to mature in the Lord. He still has work for us to do.

We are of worth. God knit us together perfectly, because He doesn't make junk. God is a God of second chances; he works with us until we get it right. An encouraging word lifts our spirits and gives us hope to keep going. When we put God first and give Him His portion, He runs our cup of blessing over. The longer we stay in our prayer rooms, the easier it is to recognize God's voice.

The presence of the Holy Spirit in us is proven by the faith we demonstrate. He is real. He is God. He is our helper, our protector, our counselor and teacher. He gives us wisdom, spiritual gifts, comfort, and so much more. Love is the perfect gift from God. It was displayed to us on the cross. God gave us His Son, Jesus, to lead us to salvation, and the Holy Spirit keeps us there. Even when we let the Lord down, He still favors us with His grace. When He says "I am who I am" that means He is all, He is everything. We need to start each day with Him.

Day Ninety

AT THE MOUNTAIN (PART TWO)

God steps into tragedies when we want to give up. God is the one to sit on the throne, not us. God is Spirit, and He's everywhere in heaven and on earth. God is not limited by time. When we take Jesus off the cross, He walks with us on this journey of life, and there are times when He carries us. When we cry, He cries with us and wraps His loving arms around us until we feel secure. When we're sick, He comforts us. When we don't know what to do, or how to do it, He shows us. He has done so much for us, we don't have proper words to thank Him. On this journey of life, we never walk alone.

***

If you're reading this and you want the restorer of brokenness and heartache to heal you, just say this simple prayer that I have written and start a journey with the Lord that will make you whole again: "Please Lord Jesus, come into my life. Forgive me of my sins and walk the path of salvation with me. I desire to be restored and I ask you for healing in my soul. Thank you for the cross. Amen."